THE LAST HORIZON

MAGGIE CUDANIN EBBINGHAUS

PUBLISHING PRESS

Copyright © ABLE Publishing Press
First published in Australia in 2024
by ABLE Publishing Press

Text Copyright © Maggie Cudanin Ebbinghaus 2025

All rights reserved. No part of this book may be used or reproduced by any means, graphic, electronic, or mechanical, including photocopying, recording, taping or by any information storage retrieval system without the written permission of the copyright owner except in the case of brief quotations embodied in critical articles and reviews.

Because of the dynamic nature of the Internet, any web addresses or links contained in this book may have changed since publication and may no longer be vaild. The views expressed in this work are solely those of the author and do not necessarily reflect the views of the publisher and the publisher hereby disclaims any responsibility for them.

 A catalogue record for this work is available from the National Library of Australia

National Library of Australia Catalogue-in-Publication data:
The Last Horizon / Maggie Cudanin Ebbinghaus

DEDICATION

To my loving parents Fernando and Soledad Cudanin, whose love and support brought me into this world.

And to my precious daughter Mycah and my son Monreo; your inspiration fuels my strength and determination every day.

To my dear grandchildren, Gideon, Azelia and Areli. Your laughter and joy light up my life and inspire me.

To my son-in-law, Lawrence, thank you for loving my daughter with all your heart.

To my daughter-in-law Floremmel, thank you for loving my son so deeply. Your love enriches our family in countless ways.

To my husband, Lothar, thank you for your unwavering support and for bringing us to Australia. Your love and inspiration have guided me to share your story.

This book is for you.

PROLOGUE

In a world swirling with uncertainties and trials, each day presents us with the opportunity to confront the formidable challenges that life lay before us. "The Last Horizon" is not just a story; it is a testament to the indomitable spirit that resides within each of us, urging us to rise and face our adversities with unwavering courage.

Challenges come from everywhere – unexpected twists that ripple through the fabric of our lives, each one donning its unique guise, be it emotional, physical or existential. They can loom large on the horizon like storm clouds, threatening to overshadow our hopes and dreams. Yet, within each challenge lies a lesson, a pathway to growth, and a chance to become stronger than we ever imagined.

We employ our personal strategies to navigate these trials, crafting tools of resilience from our experiences. Social support becomes our lifeline, as friends and family rally around us, lending their strength when ours seems insufficient. In moments when human assistance falls short, we find solace in faith, believing that divine intervention can illuminate our darkest paths.

To face our challenges is to embrace life; to attack them head-on is to wield the power of transformation. It is in the act of confronting adversity that we discover our true selves – stronger, smarter; and more capable than before. The very essence of our character is sculpted through the trials we withstand. Conversely, shying away from our challenges only feeds the shadows of cowardice and weakness, leaving us nervous, retreating into a shell that stifles our potential.

As we embark on this journey through "*The Last Horizon*," let us remember that within every struggle lies the promise of a new horizon. Each obstacle we face is not merely a hurdle to overcome, but an opportunity to redefine ourselves, to grow and to evolve.

Together, we will explore the depths of resilience, the power of unwavering faith, and the strength that emerges when we refuse to run from our challenges. Herein lies a call to action – one that beckons us to not only face our trials but to charge through them, equipped with determination and a fierce belief in our capacity to conquer. Welcome to the odyssey of resilience. Welcome to "*The Last Horizon*."

CHAPTER 1
A CHILDHOOD DEFINED BY CHALLENGES

"I am migrating to Australia!" Lothar's heart raced as he held the coveted document in his hands – a visa to migrate to Australia. Excitement bubbled within him like a pot reaching the boil, sending thrills of anticipation rushing through his veins. His eyes widened with wonder as he pictured the vast, sun-kissed landscapes, the crystal-clear waters teeming with life, and a promise of a new beginning awaiting him on the faraway continent. Lothar had dreamt of exploring new horizons beyond his homeland since he was a child.

Love Over Blood
Lothar was born in Gelsenkirchen a significant industrial city in Germany, particularly known for its coal mining and steel production. Located in the Ruhr area, it was one of the hubs of Germany's heavy industry. The city's economy was heavily reliant on these industries, which made it a target for strategic planning and later bombing during World War II.

Lothar was born in 1938, just a year before the outbreak of

THE LAST HORIZON

World War II, into a world that would be forever altered with conflict. The war stripped away the innocence of youth, leaving him to navigate a landscape scarred by chaos and despair. His father, a dedicated soldier, served his country with honour, but tragically lost his life in the harsh battles of Mariupol. This loss left an indelible mark on Lothar's childhood, shaping his early experiences and perspectives in life.

Lothar's father Otto, the 12th child of devout Catholic parents often found himself wandering away from the rigid traditions that defined his world, particularly when he met Else. Else was a spirited Protestant, her laughter ringing like wind chimes on a warm summer day.

The pair often stole moments together by the river, discussing dreams and hopes,and crafting a future painted in vibrant colours that clashed starkly with the monochrome palette of their family backgrounds.

Their love blossomed like wildflowers, untamed and full of life, but beneath the surface lingered the fear of disapproval.

When Otto decided to marry Else, the wrath of tradition fell upon him like a storm. Dismissed and disinherited, he stood at the threshold of his childhood home, heart heavy and torn asunder. His mother's eyes filled with unshed tears, would be the last he saw of his family.

With Else by his side, Otto forged a new path, building a life together against the odds. They welcomed their son, Lothar, into the world, a boy born not just of love but of rebellion against the confines of family tradition and religion.

Otto often cradled the infant, whispering promises of a life filled with freedom and choices - a life untouched by the binds of religious strife. Yet, as the war escalated, Otto felt the call of duty beckon him. Leaving Else and Lothar behind, he donned his uniform, carrying not just a weapon but a heavy heart.

MAGGIE CUDANIN EBBINGHAUS

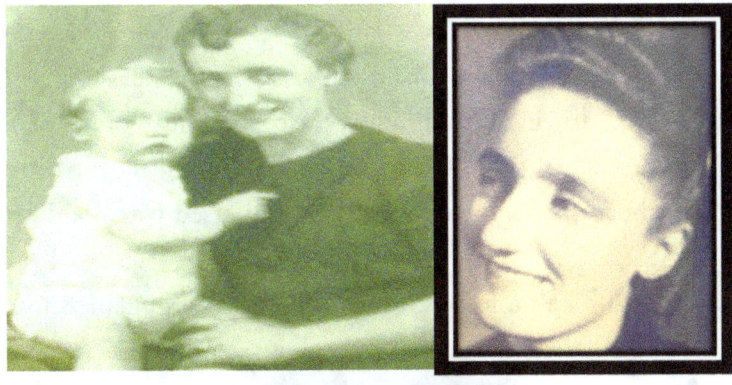

As Otto marched into the unknown, he often reminisced about his home, the laughter of his son, and his dreams of a peaceful future.

The battle fronts were brutal, but it was in Mariupol, Soviet Union (now Ukraine) that Otto met his fate. The city was occupied by German forces during World War II and experienced significant fighting and destruction. As Otto's unit fought fiercely for their cause, he felt the weight of his decisions pressing down upon him. His thoughts often drifted home to his son Lothar, whom he longed to see grow strong and free, and to Else, whose love had been his anchor.

In a tide of chaos, the burst of artillery filled the air. Otto pushed forward, driven by a mix of courage and the hope of returning to the embrace of his family. But in the cruel twist of fate, a grenade hit him on the head. He fell, calling the name of his wife "Else... Else," until his last breath.

Back in Gelsenkirchen, baby Lothar was sleeping next to his mother Else. Else was drifting into slumber, the cosy warmth of her blankets enveloping her, when a sudden noise jolted her awake. The sound of her name echoed through the stillness, interspersed with loud knocking against the wall.

Confused and half asleep, she rubbed her eyes and glanced out the window, the moonlight casting an eerie glow over the empty street. To her bewilderment, there was no one there – just the quiet of the night, amplifying the mystery of the unsettling call.

Days turned into weeks, and the strange occurrences faded into the background of her mind, replaced by the mundane rhythms of daily life. However, a gnawing anxiety lingered in her heart, whispering that something was amiss.

It wasn't until a letter was personally delivered to her by her husband's comrade – a cold, stark notification from the military – that the truth pierced through her senses like a shard of glass.

Otto had been hit by a grenade in the chaos of battle. In that moment, Else learned that the echoes she had heard were not just figments of her imagination but his desperate calls in those final moments. "Else, Else," he had cried, a haunting refrain that reverberated in her soul.

As she mourned, those two haunting syllables became a lifeline to their shared past. In her dreams, Else could almost hear him – his voice, a tender mixture of love and urgency – reaching out to her from beyond the veil.

The realisation struck her with overwhelming force. In his final moments, Otto had been calling for her; the connection between their hearts unbroken even by death.

During the war, Lothar found solace and stability in the company of his mother and grandfather Julius Drutsch who originally came from Kaliningrad East Prussia and his grandmother Helene from Lithuania. Julius and Helene were a loving couple, bound together by shared hopes and dreams, yet faced with a heartbreaking reality – they were childless.

Despite their deep desire to raise a family, fertility challenges had thwarted their plans, leaving a void in their lives that echoed with unfulfilled aspirations.

Amidst their longing, fate intervened when Else entered their lives. Born out of wedlock, she was a baby in need of a family; her French birthmother, recognising the challenges of raising a child alone, made the difficult decision to put her up for adoption.

This choice though painful, opened the door to a new beginning for both Else and the childless couple. When Julius and Helene learned of the opportunity to adopt Else, their hearts swelled with hope. They welcomed her into their home, seeing her not just as a child but the embodiment of their dreams.

From the moment they held her, they felt an instant bond as if this tiny being was meant to complete their family. As Else grew, she became the light in Julius' and Helene's lives. They poured their love into her. Though Else was born under different circumstances, she was embraced as their own.

However, in Germany, the law dictates that adoptive parents must reveal the truth of an adoption to their child when they reach the age of 21. For Julius and Helene, this moment loomed with a mixture of anticipation and trepidation. They had raised Else with unwavering love, treating her as their own flesh and blood, and now faced the responsibility of sharing the story of her origins.

Julius took a deep breath, his heart pounding, while Helene reached out to hold Else's hand, a gesture of solidarity and love. As they unfolded the truth of Else's adoption, they spoke not only of her origins but also emphasised the depth of their love and commitment to her and to her son Lothar.

Their unwavering commitment continued until the end of their lives. Lothar's grandparents offered support and care, lending a sense of continuity and family amidst chaos. Julius and Helene loved Lothar as their own flesh and blood and taught him the importance of a strong work ethic.   Julius became Lothar's role model in life.

Helene - Else - Julius

As a little boy, he witnessed the world around him being torn apart by the ravages of war. The cacophony of bombings, the wails of anguish and the ever-present scent of smoke that hung heavily in the air. Lothar was evacuated from place to place and from cellar to cellar. He saw hundreds of people being transported on goods trains to Mauthausen. Despite his tender age, Lothar learned quickly that survival demanded resilience and resourcefulness.

In the aftermath of bombings that left buildings as mere shells of their former selves, Lothar took it upon himself to scavenge for scraps of metal and other recyclables, amidst the rubble and ruins. With determination etched in his young features, he braved the dangers that lurked in the debris, driven by a singular purpose – to help his widowed mother make ends meet.

Dust-covered and determined at seven-years-old, Lothar scoured the devastated landscape, sifting through the remnants of once vibrant homes and businesses. With a sense of purpose beyond his years, Lothar meticulously scoured the debris, his small hands searching for bricks that survived the devastation. Each brick tells a story, and Lothar treated them with reverence, using a tommy hawk to clean them of grime and dust, revealing their original colour and texture. With determination, he arranged the reclaimed bricks into neat palettes of one thousand, creating small fortresses of his labour amid the chaos. Once stacked and sorted, Lothar found eager buyers, selling the bricks to those looking to rebuild their lives and their homes.

His entrepreneurial spirit did not stop there; he also gathered kindling from the remnants of fallen wood, preparing bundles to sell for warmth during the cold nights. Additionally, Lothar had an eye for the valuable scraps often overlooked by adults. He collected lengths of copper wire, carefully untangling them from the wreckage and saving them from rust. With each piece he gathered, he sold them at the local scrap dealer, earning a few coins that represented his hard work and resilience. He dodged broken glass, twisted metal, and moments of despair, clinging to hope like a lifeline as he gathered whatever salvageable items he could find. Each discarded piece held the promise of a few coins that could buy a loaf of bread.

CHAPTER 2
A JOURNEY BEYOND THE RUINS

Days turned into weeks, and weeks turned into months, yet Lothar's resolve never wavered. His small hands grew calloused, and his spirit, though tested, remained unbroken. The scars of war marked not only the landscape but also his being, shaping him into a boy wise beyond his years. In a world turned upside down by war, Lothar's resourcefulness and spirit shone brightly as he transformed destruction into opportunity, embodying hope for a future that slowly began to rebuild.

From a young age, Lothar also exhibited an insatiable curiosity for the world around him, often found gazing at maps and dreaming of distant lands. His heart raced at the thought of adventure. Whether it was navigating rugged mountain trails or speeding down a winding bike path, his innate desire for exploration led him to immerse himself in nature, often spending weekends hiking in the hills or biking through the verdant forests embracing the thrill of the unknown.

Every day after school, he would make his way through the bustling streets of his quaint town, his satchel slung over his shoulder and a skip in his step. Upon reaching the colourful market square, Lothar would find his mother Else amidst a bustle of vendors, their stalls adorned with an array of fresh fruits and vegetables organised by Else's new husband Bill.

With a smile that could light up the darkest corner, his mother would welcome him with open arms. Through the mundane yet meaningful interactions at the market, Lothar's world expanded beyond the confines of the schoolyard.

"Apples! Fresh apples! You'll get a discount if you buy one dozen!" Lothar yelled out.

With nimble fingers, he deftly arranged the fruits, ensuring each one was perfectly positioned, showcasing their freshness. His pride was evident as he picked up a shiny red apple, holding it up for potential buyers. "Try this one! It's the juiciest in the market!" The apple glistened in the light, almost as if it were winking at the onlookers.

Lothar beamed with pride as he packed up the last of the fresh produce at the bustling market, the scent of the ripe fruits and vegetables lingering in the air. He had spent the day assisting his mother and stepfather, learning the ins and outs of the market system, and even helping customers find the freshest goods.

His hard work didn't go unnoticed; among the many faces in the crowd was his stepfather, Bill, who watched him from a distance, a look of astonishment in his eyes.

Bill was a sturdy man with rough calloused hands, worn from years of labour. He obliged Lothar to read books and summarise the story to him before going to bed. This continued until Lothar fell in love with books. He had always encouraged Lothar to embrace responsibility but often found it hard to express his pride. Today, he felt a wave of admiration for the boy's determination and diligence. He wanted to give him something special.

Bill wandered through the remnants of crumbled buildings. Among the debris, he stumbled upon a rusted bicycle frame, half-buried in the rubble. Its once vibrant colour now dulled by layers of rust and neglect. Determined to breathe new life into it, he meticulously cleaned the frame, scrubbing away at the corrosion that had accumulated over time. Each stroke of his brush revealed the metal's original contours and potential. After ensuring it was free from rust, he carefully selected a fresh coat of paint applying it with precision. The transformation was remarkable. A spark of inspiration ignited within him. Determined to revive the bike, Bill scavenged nearby for rubber tires, finding a pair that fit perfectly. But as he inspected the wheels, he realised there were no inner tubes. Inner tubes were not available anywhere in the village after World War II.

The harsh reality of scarcity weighed on him, but he refused to give up. With a resourceful spirit, he remembered he had an old water hose. He filled the hose with sand, shaping it to fit snugly inside the wheels. He tied it tightly with wire, creating a makeshift inner tube; a testament to his ingenuity.

On a chilly Christmas morning, Lothar's eyes widened as his stepfather presented the bicycle to him. "This is my Christmas gift for you, son." Lothar could hardly believe it; his stepfather had surprised him with a gift he had only dreamed of receiving. The bicycle was not just a means of transportation, it was a symbol of love and effort, built with care by Bill's hands.

When the inner tube finally became available, Bill wasted no time in getting to work on the bicycle. Excitement coursed through him as he carefully removed the wheel, his hands deftly manoeuvring the tools he'd gathered for the task. With focus and determination, he detached the water hose filled with sand and skilfully inserted the new inner tube, ensuring it was properly seated within the

tyre to prevent any future mishaps. After reassembling the wheels, Bill inflated the tubes, watching as it took place, filling with air beneath his careful touch. The familiar sound of the air pump punctuated the moment, signalling that the bicycle was almost ready for its first ride.

The bicycle represented not only freedom and joy but also the acknowledgment of Lothar's efforts and potential, marking a significant chapter in their relationship and Lothar's journey ahead.

One unforgettable journey started on a bright summer morning when Lothar couldn't shake the thrill bubbling in his chest. As the final school bell rang, releasing Lothar into the warm embrace of summer, excitement surged through him.

For six glorious weeks, he would be free to explore the Black Forest with his trusty bicycle as his only companion. With a backpack filled with essentials and a heart bursting with adventure, he set off into the sunlit world.

Navigating the scenic countryside, Lothar spent his days cycling through lush fields, winding lanes and quaint villages, each turn revealing new sights and sounds. He breathed in the fresh air, filled with the scent of blooming wildflowers and sun-warmed earth. It was liberation in every sense.

At night when the sun dipped into the horizon and stars began to twinkle in the velvet sky, Lothar needed a place to rest. He slept under the stars pitching his tent in the meadows with soft grass, or at times in the welcoming shelters of hostels in the sleepy towns he encountered. But as his journey progressed, he wanted to try something different – something that connected him with the local communities.

One evening, as dusk settled in the small village of Edingen, Lothar spotted a charming farmhouse surrounded by towering trees and fields of golden wheat. A warm light spilled from the windows, and the scent of fresh bread wafted through the air, teasing his senses. He decided to knock on the door. With a mix of excitement and anxiety, Lothar approached the door and raised his hand, knocking gently.

Moments later, a kind-faced farmer opened the door, surprised to see a young boy standing there with a hopeful expression.

"Good evening, sir," Lothar began, his voice steady. "My name is Lothar, I'm travelling on my bicycle, and I was wondering if you might allow me to sleep in your barn? I can chop your firewood in the morning," Lothar continued. "No need to chop my firewood, young man," the kind farmer said. "Just come in, spend the night in my spare room and join us for dinner." In the morning, Herr Johannes offered him a hearty breakfast of fresh bread, butter and jam.

Over the meal, they exchanged stories – Lothar shared tales of his adventures, and Mr. Johannes recounted the history of the land and its changing seasons. With full bellies and newfound friendship, Lothar thanked Mr. Johannes and pedalled off, ready for the next leg of his adventure.

After every few hours of riding, Lothar stopped for a break. He stretched his legs and pulled out his provisions relishing the simple joy of eating fresh bread and cheese in the great outdoors. Once he finished his lunch, he grabbed the box camera and snapped a photo of a charming scene - the woods, wildflowers and wildlife. It took him more than two weeks to reach the Black Forest.

The air was fresh and crisp as Lothar stepped deeper into the beckoning embrace of the Black Forest. Sunlight filtered through the thick canopy of oak trees, European beech, Silver Fir, and other deciduous conifers creating a mosaic of light and shadows on the soft forest floor. His heart raced with excitement as he followed the sound of the rushing water, an elusive melody that promised discovery.

After a short hike, Lothar stumbled upon the breathtaking Triberg waterfall cascading down rugged rocks, the water sparkling like diamonds as it danced and swirled. Overwhelmed by the beauty, he quickly set his camera on a nearby stump, to capture the scene in all its glory. The roar of the water enveloped him, drowning out the world as he focused on framing the perfect shot.

Lothar poised himself, ready to capture the perfect shot with his camera, the shutter almost pressing under his finger. Just as he prepared to click, misfortune struck; his footing slipped, and he slid down the moss-covered cliff. The slick moss clung to the rough surface of the rock, but it offered little traction, and he tumbled downward with a rush of adrenaline, the world blurring around him.

He landed with a splash in the first layer of the cascading waterfall, the cold water rising swiftly to his neck. Panic surged through him as he frantically searched for his camera only to realise it was gone, swallowed by the rushing current. Feeling the weight of his loss, he took a moment to gather his resolve, eyeing the tumultuous water around him.

Amidst the chaos, something caught his attention – a sturdy vine that hung down from the overhanging edge above. Instinct kicked in as he reached for it, gripping it tightly to steady himself. The vine felt rough and strong in his hands, a lifeline in the swirling water. Carefully, he began to pull himself upward, inching against the current and leveraging the vine to regain his footing.

Heart pounding, Lothar carefully pulled himself up, inch by inch, until he could find solid ground on the hillside once again. He collapsed onto the soft earth, breathing heavily, the reality of his narrow escape sinking in. As he picked himself up, dusting off the leaves, sand and dirt, he felt a renewed determination. This experience had been more than a scare, it had ignited the fire within him to explore and to face challenges head-on with a full heart. With a cautious but eager spirit, Lothar continued onward, ready for whatever lay ahead.

Lothar started pedalling again. On a sun-drenched afternoon, he stumbled upon two teenagers Rudolf and Hans who were also travelling on their bicycle along the Baden-Wurttemberg highway.

Their camaraderie was palpable, and before long, Lothar found himself swept into their fold, sharing stories and laughter. They started singing their favourite boy scouting folk songs. As the dusk descended, the trio made their way to the serene edge of Lake Titisee. The waters shimmered with hues of orange and pink, mirroring the sunset sky.

Enthralled, they set up camp beneath a canopy of stars, the cool breeze carrying the sweet scent of pine. The following morning, the tranquil waters of the Titisee shimmered invitingly in the morning sun. "Let's swim the length of the lake," Rudolf suggested. Without a second thought, they all plunged into the refreshing depths.

For a while, the swim was exhilarating. They laughed and splashed, the cool water invigorating against their sun-warmed skin. However, after about half an hour of swimming, Lothar began to struggle. His legs, fatigued from the exertion, soon betrayed him. Shooting pain surged through his right leg, cramping painfully.

Panic momentarily set in as Lothar realised he wasn't going to make it to the shore on his own. He raised his arm signalling for help. Instantly, the two young men recognised his distress. Without hesitation, they swiftly made their way back to him. "Hold on! We're coming!" Hans shouted as they swam towards Lothar.

They reached him just in time, offering their support. While Rudolf wrapped an arm around Lothar, Hans kicked vigorously to navigate them safely back to solid ground. "That was quite the swim!" Rudolf chuckled, his expression a mix of concern and amusement. Lothar smiled, realising that what had started as a fun day at the lake could have easily turned into something serious. Once Lothar recovered from his ordeal, they all sat around the campfire once again, the mood lightening with laughter, stories and folk songs.

Lothar woke early the next morning, the sun filtering through his tent. He felt a sense of gratitude and relief after the harrowing experience of almost drowning in Lake Titisee, where his friends had come to his rescue just in time. As he prepared for his bike ride, memories of the event lingered in his mind, reminding him of the bond he shared with his new friends. After checking his bike ensuring that the tyres were inflated and the chain well lubricated, Lothar mounted his bike. He set off down the winding path that framed the serene Lake Titisee, the water reflecting the cloudless blue sky.

As he pedalled, the gentle sound of rustling leaves and the chirping birds accompanied him, creating a soundtrack of nature's tranquillity. He felt a mix of emotions, a sense of liberation on the open road, paired with a lingering awareness of how precious life is.

With each turn of the pedals, Lothar embraced the freedom of the ride, the wind against his face and the vibrant surroundings of the Black Forest enveloping him. The memory of his friends' support played in his mind, fuelling his determination and appreciation for the present moment. Today, he was not just a cyclist traversing familiar paths, he was a survivor, a friend and a seeker of new adventures, enjoying life one ride at a time.

THE LAST HORIZON

On his way back home cycling for 16 days, and with a hundred kilometres still to go, his spirits had begun to wane. With each passing hour, the weight of his situation bore down on him more heavily. He had run out money, and it had been far too long since he last had a proper meal.

The horizon stretched out endlessly before him, a shimmering mirage of heat rising from the asphalt. He could not see any farmhouses from the road. Just when he began to despair, he spotted something vibrant among the muted brown and greens of the landscape: a newly – harvested cornfield. His heart quickened at the sight. He approached the field cautiously, scanning the area to ensure no one was watching. With desperation clawing at his insides, he knelt among the remnants of the harvest, the earth still warm from the sun.

He began to collect grains of corn, fingers trembling with both fatigue and anticipation. Each handful he gathered felt like a treasure, a life-saving gift from the earth. As he held the precious grains, he thought about how a simple kernel could transform into sustenance – a meal to quench his gnawing hunger. He sat down upon the earth leaning against the fence at the edge of the field.

He gave in to his hunger and began to chew on the fresh grains savouring their natural sweetness. With each handful, he felt strength returning to his limbs, a warmth spreading through him as he savoured the simple yet profound pleasure of having found food when he needed it most. The handfuls of corn were fulfilling enough to give him the energy to continue his journey until he finally reached home. Lothar learned lessons not only from the beauty of the world around him but also from the challenges he faced along the way.

The very next morning, he gathered his school supplies with a sigh. As he pedalled his bicycle to attend school, a mix of excitement and anxiety bubbled within him. Arriving at school, Lothar was greeted by familiar faces and the chatter of classmates eager to share their own summer adventures.

The buzz of energy lifted his spirits, reminding him that even though the carefree days of summer had ended, a new chapter was beginning. With his heart full of memories and the determination to face the challenges ahead, Lothar stepped into the school building ready to embrace the year ahead.

Lothar and His Bicycle in 1948

At school, Lothar sat at his desk, his fingers gripping a pencil as he stared at the chalkboard, the scritch-scratch of his teacher's voice fading into a dull hum. Mr. Muller, their stern and unwavering Mathematics instructor had just returned from his service in the war, his once warm eyes now steely and distant. His presence commanded respect, and his reputation for discipline preceded him like a shadow.

The classroom was hushed as Mr. Muller prowled amongst the rows of students, his gaze sweeping over them with a sharpness that made even the bravest quail. Lothar could feel the weight of his scrutiny, the expectation of excellence pressing down upon him like a leaden blanket. When Mr. Muller called upon him to answer a question, Lothar felt his heart skip a beat.

The words seemed to blur on the page before him, his mind a jumble of confusion and fear. As he stammered out a reply, Mr. Muller's patience snapped like a taut string, his right hand reaching out to grasp his hair in a cruel vice-like grip.

A gasp rippled through the classroom as Lothar winced in pain, the sting of his reprimand burning into his very being. And then, with a swift motion that left Mr. Muller's hand smarting, his left hand connected with Lothar's skin in a sharp slap, the sound echoing in the stunned silence of the room. For a moment, time seemed to stand still, the air thick with tension and disbelief. Lothar's eyes filled with tears, a mix of shame and defiance swirling within him like a storm.

Lothar stood at the crossroads of his future his gaze fixed on the narrow path that diverged from the well-trodden road of higher education. He quit school before completing the six years of studies. The lure of academia held no sway over his young heart. The call of the unknown, the pull of independence, whispered seductively in his ear, beckoning him towards a different path. He opted to become a bricklayer.

Becoming a bricklayer in Germany in 1951 required a combination of technical skills, physical abilities and personal qualities, reflecting the construction practices and economic conditions of the time.

In his apprenticeship, he learned the knowledge of different bricklaying methods, masonry skills reading blueprints, mathematical skills, spatial awareness, problem-solving skills, safety practices, knowledge of materials, teamwork and communication, work ethics and construction techniques. He also learned basic arithmetic in order to perform calculations for measurements, material quantities and costs. He was also required to complete the apprenticeship program.

Fourteen-year-old Lothar stood at the edge of the construction site, his heart racing with anticipation and a hint of dread. The winter clouds enveloped the horizon while Lothar was looking at the half-built structure that loomed before him. Today marked the beginning of his apprenticeship as a bricklayer. Lothar was determined to obey his foreman.

However, the thought of climbing to the fourth level on a rickety makeshift ladder made his stomach churn. He glanced at the towering structure, its walls slowly taking form, and swallowed hard. "Get to work, Lothar!" called out Mr. Zimmerman, the foreman, a burly man with a weathered face and a voice that echoed like thunder. "We need mortar on the fourth level!" Swallowing his nervousness, Lothar nodded.

He watched as other apprentices moved with agility and purpose, hauling heavy buckets of mortar and bricks.

Determined to do his job, he lifted the heavy bucket filled with mortar onto his shoulders, the coarse gritty substance shifting slightly as he balanced it. The pain from the weight was immediate, but he steeled himself. Each step he took toward the ladder felt like a journey toward his future.

He approached the timber ladder – a patchwork of salvaged wood, its surface rough and splintered. It leaned precariously against the side of the building, the higher rungs swaying slightly in the cold morning breeze. Lothar placed one foot on the first rung, testing it cautiously, his heart pounding in his chest as he hoisted the bucket higher, gripping it tightly as he ascended. The wind whistled past him; the sound mingled with the raucous calls of his co-workers below. Time seemed to stretch as he climbed, focusing intently on the next rung, the next step.

"Keep going, Lothar! You're doing great! A voice from below called out, and for a fleeting moment, encouragement replaced his fear. After what felt like an eternity, he reached the fourth level. Lothar breathed a sigh of relief as he carefully descended the last rung, his feet finding solid ground again. He set the bucket down, trembling slightly from the exertion. "Now let's get to work on those bricks." As the sun climbed higher, they began the delicate dance of laying bricks, the rhythm of their work creating a melody of hammers and laughter. Weeks turned into months and Lothar became fascinated with the art of construction, the alchemy of turning raw materials into structures that stood as testaments to human ingenuity and craftsmanship. He embarked on an apprenticeship as a bricklayer, eager to learn the ropes of a trade at the age of 14, promised both challenge and fulfillment.

From the crack of dawn until the sun dipped below the horizon, Lothar immersed himself in the world of mortar, bricks and sweat, each day bringing new lessons and experiences that shaped him into a craftsman of remarkable ability.

The duties that awaited him each morning were as varied as they were demanding. Mixing mortar by hand, the gritty mixture of sand, cement, and water under his fingers, Lothar learned the delicate balance of consistency and precision that lay at the heart of quality masonry.

The rhythmic motion of his arms as he worked the mortar into a smooth paste became second nature. But it was the task of carrying mortar on his shoulders that truly tested Lothar's mettle. Ascending makeshift ladders of wood and rope, each step precarious and laden with the weight of his burden, he trudged upwards to higher levels of the building, his muscles straining against the pull of gravity.

With each load he hoisted, each bead of sweat that trickled down his brow, Lothar felt a sense of accomplishment that transcended the physical exertion – a deep-rooted pride in his ability to conquer the challenges set before him.

One afternoon, as Lothar trudged across the construction site, the heavy bag of lime slung over his shoulder felt like a boulder, but he pushed through, focused on his task. Suddenly, the strap slipped, and the bag plummeted to the ground, bursting open upon impact. A fine cloud of white powder erupted swirling around him like a ghostly mist.

Before he could react, a sharp sting invaded his right eye, searing with an intensity that blotted out the bustling sounds of the site. Panic surged through him as he stumbled, his heart racing, but fortunately, after a frantic splash of water from a nearby bucket, he found relief. Though his vision blurred, and discomfort lingered, he realized with a mix of dread and relief that, against all odds, he would not lose his sight.

As days turned into weeks and weeks to months, Lothar learned not just the physical demands of his trade but the camaraderie that tied the workers together. He laughed with the older apprentices, listened to their stories, and even earned the respect of Mr. Zimmerman when he successfully mixed his first batch of mortar.

After two gruelling years of apprenticeship under the blazing sun in summer and the bitter cold winters, Lothar decided to step away from the dusty confines of the construction site, his hands calloused yet skilled from the art of bricklaying. The towering walls he helped build whispered tales of stability and permanence, but his heart yearned for the thrill of an open sea.

While waiting for the opportunity to fulfill his dream of becoming a sailor, Lothar started learning the Greek-Roman wrestling. Being competitive, he prepared for the wrestling match in the village square. The sun hung high in the sky, casting a warm glow over the cobblestone square, which was bustling with villagers gathered to witness the event. The atmosphere was vibrant, filled with the chatter of excited spectators, laughter, and the unmistakable sounds of proud cheers.

THE LAST HORIZON

Having trained tirelessly, Lothar felt a rush of confidence as he remembered the strength and techniques he had learned. But today, there was an added spark of determination in his heart – several young ladies from the village gathered to watch. Their laughter and glances stirred something deep within him, igniting a fierce desire to win and impress them.

The competitors faced off, muscles tense and minds focused. As the whistle blew, Lothar sprang into action. He utilised his training, executing a series of moves with precision, grappling and twisting to gain the upper hand. The crowd erupted with cheers as he manoeuvred gracefully, his movements fluid and strategic. With every hold and throw, he could feel the energy of the onlookers urging him on. Each cheer amplified his resolve. He was not just fighting for victory but for the attention and admiration of those watching – in particular, the young ladies whose smiles fuelled his determination.

As the match progressed, Lothar's opponent showed fierce resistance, but when Lothar saw the young ladies, he dug deep, drawing on both his physical strength and mental focus. Finally, with a determined burst of energy, he executed a well-timed throw, pinning his opponent to the ground.

The crowd erupted into cheers and applause, the sound ringing in his ears like music. Breathless but exhilarated, Lothar stood tall, a grin breaking across his face as he raised his arms in victory. He glanced toward the group of young ladies, their smiles wide and eyes sparkling with admiration. In that moment, he felt a swell of pride and joy, knowing that he not only won the match but also captured their attention.

As he turned fifteen, his ambitions expanded, and the call of the sea beckoned to him with the same intensity. He envisioned life on the open water, working aboard ships, where each day promised new horizons and fresh discoveries.

The idea of seafaring captivated him, promising not only to traverse the globe but also the opportunity to connect with diverse cultures and experiences.

After World War II, working on ships in Germany was an appealing prospect, influenced by several socio-economic and cultural factors. Germany's economy was in the early stages of recovery, particularly due to the Marshall Plan. The Marshall Plan, officially known as the European Recovery Program (ERP), was an American initiative launched in 1948 to aid Western Europe's economic recovery after the war. Named after Secretary of State George C. Marshall, the plan aimed to rebuild war-torn regions, remove trade barriers, modernise industry, and improve European prosperity to prevent the spread of communism.

The maritime industry was essential for trade and economic revitalisation, making jobs in shipping attractive as demand for goods and transportation surged. The allure of the sea and adventure drew many young men like Lothar to maritime careers.

Sailors often romanticised their work as offering freedom, exploration and the chance to visit distant lands, which contrasted with the more static and predictable life on land. The popularity of sea shanties and sailor's songs like 'Seeman' (Sailor's Song) by German composer and musician Heino or 'Aloha Oe' which originated in New Zealand or the German version of La Paloma originally composed by Spanish Sebastian Yradier in the 19th century among others, ignited Lothar's curiosity to become a seafarer.

After World War II, Germany was divided into East German Democratic Republic and West (Federal Republic of Germany). East Germans had limited rights concerning travels and passport.

Lothar, being a citizen of West Germany had no trouble acquiring a passport from the Passamt in the district of Gelsenkirchen. He held his passport tightly in his hand, the weight of it symbolising not just a document, but his dreams of adventure and freedom. "I'm ready mum! I'm going to Hamburg to find work on a ship!" He beamed, eyes shining with excitement.

But his stepfather, towering and concerned, snatched the passport from him, scowling. "You're too young to work on a ship, Lothar. It's dangerous out there," he barked, dismissing his dreams like a fleeting shadow. Lothar's heart crumpled at the words, a heavy sadness settling in his chest as he watched the possibility of finding himself dissolve into disappointment.

In that moment, the vibrant horizons of the sea felt impossibly far away, and the reality of his stepfather's grip tightened around his aspirations. Feeling compelled to explore other options, Lothar remembered his friend Norbert's father Mr. Wagner, a stern yet fair supervisor at the local underground mines.

Lothar had always admired the man's work ethic and knowledge, so he decided to reach out, hoping he might understand his situation and offer a solution. With a steady heartbeat, Lothar approached Mr. Wagner. He explained his plight, emphasising his eagerness to work and learn despite being underage.

Mr. Wagner listened intently, his brow furrowing in thought. After a moment, he leaned back and regarded Lothar with a discerning look. "You know, this job isn't for the faint-hearted, lad," he said, his voice firm but not unkind. "But if you are really serious about working hard and learning, I can consider giving you a chance – just this once."

Lothar was relieved and excited. He knew it wouldn't be easy, as he would have to prove himself, but he was ready for the challenge. With a mixture of gratitude and determination, Lothar was prepared to dive into the tough but rewarding work ahead, knowing this was the start of a path that could lead him to greater independence and responsibility.

By law, 15-year-olds are not allowed to work in the coal mines that lay nestled 800 metres underground, a world shrouded in darkness, danger and toil.

As he descended into the depths of the earth for the first time, the cool damp air enveloped him like a heavy cloak, the echoes of the underground train, mingling with the distant murmurs of his fellow miners. The dim glow of his carbide lantern cast long shadows upon the craggy walls, illuminating a world steeped in grit and resilience.

Each shift began with the descent – a slow methodical journey down into the bowels of the earth. From the 800-metre point of descent, Lothar and his comrades boarded a small underground train that rattled and clanked its way through the tunnels, carrying them three kilometres into the heart of the mine. The cold, damp walls of rock seemed to press in closer with each passing metre, a constant reminder of the weight of the earth above.

Upon reaching their destination, the miners disembarked and began the next leg of their journey on foot. Walking through narrow passageways barely wide enough for a man to pass, they struggled to navigate the labyrinthine tunnels.

The true test of their resolve awaited them further ahead. To reach the actual workplace, they had to crawl on their bellies through cramped spaces, their bodies contorted and pressed against the unforgiving rock.

The rough stones tore at their clothes and skin, leaving a trail of scratches and bruises. And then came the final descent – a harrowing slide on their backs down crevices that seemed to plunge into the very heart of the earth. With heart pounding and breath held tight, Lothar lowered himself into the darkness. At last, they reached the bottom, where the dim light of their carbide lamps revealed the coal seams waiting to be unearthed.

Day after day, Lothar laboured alongside grizzled veterans of the mines, his youthful vigour a stark contrast to their weathered faces and calloused hands. He learned the rules quickly. His nimble fingers working deftly to lift the 50-pound hammer, his keen eyes scanning the darkened tunnels for signs of danger.

Life in the coal mines was unforgiving, demanding both strength of body and will. Lothar's muscles ached from the ceaseless scraping of coal and loading onto the underground trains passing behind the coal miners, his lungs filled with the thick miasma of coal dust that hung heavy in the air. His strong set of teeth were the only white part of his body after a long day's work.

Lothar's experience in the coal mines left an indelible mark on his outlook in life, shaping his perspective in profound ways. Working in the coal mines exposed him to the unrelenting demands of manual labour and the necessity of perseverance in the face of adversity. Through the physical toil and mental fortitude required in the mines, Lothar gained a deep appreciation for the value of hard work and the dignity that comes from overcoming challenges through sheer determination.

Lothar trudged through the coal mines, his determination slowly suffocating under the weight of exhaustion and despair. The suffocating darkness of the shafts had worn him down, and three months of gruelling shifts, he finally made the decision to leave it all behind.

With only a few Deutsche Marks in his pocket, he set off hoping to reunite with his best friend Diether, who now worked in Sweden.

CHAPTER 3
BOUND FOR NEW HORIZONS

As he travelled, the sound of a crackling radio caught his ear in a small diner. He froze, his heart sinking as the announcer reported a devastating gas explosion in the mines – the grim news of 400 lives lost painted a bleak picture of what could have been his fate. Overwhelmed by a mix of grief and relief, Lothar hurried onwards towards Sweden, clutching a thin thread of hope and friendship that now felt like his only lifeline.

With so few Deutsche Marks in his pocket, Lothar had to rely on unconventional methods to reach his destination. He resorted to hitchhiking, using the kindness of strangers to propel him on his journey. From his hometown in Southern Germany, he hitched rides all the way to Northern Germany and then onwards to Denmark, his heart brimming with excitement of the adventures that awaited him.

Upon reaching Denmark, Lothar seized an opportunity to board a boat bound for Malmoe, Sweden. The sea air filled his lungs, the wind in his short curly hair a harbinger of the new experiences that awaited him on foreign shores. However, his joy was short-lived when he encountered an unforeseen obstacle upon arrival.

THE LAST HORIZON

As he faced the immigration officer in Sweden, hope turned to disappointment as he was informed that he did not have the necessary documentation to enter the country legally. With little money to spare and no visa to work as he had hoped, Lothar's dreams of exploring Sweden and to find work there, crumbled before his eyes.

Dejected and with no other option, Lothar found himself in a difficult situation. The immigration authorities made the decision to deport him back to where he came from. As he boarded the boat back to Copenhagen, he reflected on the lessons learned from his failed adventure.

Upon his arrival at the Copenhagen pier, his mind was clouded with uncertainty. With a backpack heavy with essentials, he navigated his way through the bustling pier to find respite in the heart of the city. Boarding the tram bound for town, Lothar realised he had no Danish Krone (DKK) to purchase a ticket.

As the conductor approached, his stern gaze locked on Lothar, irritation flickered in his eyes. Lothar, unable to explain his predicament in a foreign language, felt the weight of apprehension settle upon him. Just as the tension threatened to escalate, an unexpected saviour emerged – an elderly man, clad in an overcoat and a kind smile. Without a word, the old man gestured to Lothar to sit back as he approached the conductor, offering to pay for the young traveller's fare.

Time seemed to freeze as gratitude flooded Lothar's heart. As the train rumbled along the tracks, Lothar opened up to the old man about his aspirations of finding work in Sweden. The old man listened intently, his eyes reflecting a past filled with experiences and learnings. Moved by Lothar's determination and sincerity, the old man began to impart valuable advice on the legalities of entering Sweden for work.

With patience and care, he guided Lothar through the steps and procedures required. In a gesture of unparalleled generosity, the old man reached into his pocket and withdrew a sum of money, pressing it gently into Lothar's hand. "To help you on your journey." He spoke softly, his voice carrying a weight of compassion that touched Lothar's soul. Gratitude overwhelmed Lothar as he looked at the old man's eyes. With the old man's help, Lothar was able to legally enter Sweden.

The second time Lothar stepped off the ship, the crisp Swedish air wrapped around him like a chilly embrace. Armed only with his friend's last known address in bustling Stockholm, he belied his mounting worry. After knocking on the door, the new tenant informed him that his friend has moved deep into the logging forests, leaving Lothar stranded in the city.

As sunset painted the sky with shades of orange and purple, he wandered along the unfamiliar streets searching for a place to rest. Suddenly, a large rubbish bin caught his eye – a peculiar refuge partly filled with sand and discarded cartons. With nowhere else to turn and exhaustion weighing him down, he curled up inside, the faint smell of refuse mingling with the forest's fresh scent carried in the evening breeze.

Under the stars, Lothar closed his eyes, thoughts drifting to the logging area where his friend now lived. Perhaps tomorrow would bring a fresh new start.

Yet for now, amid the remnants of the city's bustle, he found a moment of peace in the most unlikely of shelters.

The following day, he found a job as a dishwasher. Lothar's role as a dishwasher in a large restaurant was a physically demanding one. Every day, he faced the daunting task of washing hundreds of items of crockery and cutlery all by hand, as dishwashing machines were not yet a common feature in kitchens in 1955.

Upon arriving at the restaurant, Lothar would quickly don his apron, ready to tackle the relentless flow of dirty dishes. The cuisine was popular, and during peak hours, the kitchen was filled with the sounds of clattering pots and pans along with the lively chatter of servers. As plates, glasses and silverware piled up, Lothar became engrossed in a rhythm that combined speed and precision.

Without the aid of modern dishwashers, Lothar relied entirely on his hands. He would soak each item in hot, soapy water scrubbing away remnants of food with diligence. He observed how much expensive food went to waste. Lothar's hands often bore the marks of his labour; roughened palms from handling abrasive sponges and warm water. He understood the importance of cleanliness in the restaurant industry; every plate had to shine, presenting the food in its best light to the patrons.

As a dishwasher, he was responsible for ensuring that all kitchenware remained spotless and ready for use, while also assisting the chefs and kitchen staff with food preparation, peeling vegetables, descaling fish, dressing chicken and organising ingredients.

Lothar faced challenges in the kitchen. The workload was intense especially during busy service times. The sound of clinking silverware and the rush of staff in and out of the kitchen created an atmosphere of urgency. Although he sometimes felt fatigue setting in, Lothar took pride in his work, recognising it as a vital part of the culinary experience.

He learned to pace himself effectively, so he could keep up with the demands and still maintain the high standards expected of his position. Lothar's role also fostered camaraderie among his coworkers. Despite the intense hustle he often shared brief moments of humour and conversation with chefs and waitstaff while working in the dish pit.

These interactions bolstered his spirits and helped him feel a sense of belonging in an unfamiliar country. In the restaurant, Lothar quickly adapted to the fast-paced environment. Each day, as he scrubbed dishes and prepared meals, he found inspiration in the stories whispered by the walls of the restaurant, dreaming of the vast horizons yet to be explored.

He lived in a charming youth hostel that had once been a sailing ship, its wooden decks and nautical décor evoking a sense of adventure that stirred his imagination.

After six months, Lothar felt a growing restlessness, a yearning to step beyond the confines of the hostel and the rhythm of his current life. He decided to take a leap of faith and set his sights on Hamburg, a bustling port city that promised new opportunities and the chance to work on an actual ship. The decision filled him with excitement and trepidation, but he was determined to pursue his ambition to see the world by working on ships.

Upon arriving in Hamburg, the city's vibrant energy enveloped him. The shipyards buzzed with activity, and the salty air carried the scent of adventure. Lothar kept on searching until he found a position on a ship as a mess boy – a role that would not only provide him with income but also immerse him in the maritime lifestyle he had longed for.

The morning sun glinted off the gentle waves as Lothar stood at the dock, feeling the thrill of possibility coursing through him. He had landed a job on the *Esso-Frankfurt,* a sturdy vessel known for its reliability in the shipping industry. The ship's vibrant colours and imposing structure filled him with a sense of pride and anticipation, a tangible symbol of the hard work he had yearned for.

As he stepped aboard, the smell of salt air mixed with the scent of oil and wood engulfed him, reminding him of the sea's vastness and the adventures that awaited. The crew welcomed him with friendly nods, their camaraderie palpable as they prepared for departure.

Lothar felt as though he was stepping into a new world, one filled with duties, responsibility, and the camaraderie of the sea. As the ship began to leave the harbour, the engines roared into life; and Lothar clasped the railing, his excitement mounting with each passing moment.

The gentle sway of the vessel beneath him was both exhilarating an comforting, as if the ship were embracing him for the journey ahead. He gazed out at the shore receding into the distance, where familiar landmarks became mere silhouette on the horizon.

The salty breeze whipped through his curly hair, and Lothar's heart raced with the thoughts of exploration and discovery. The ocean stretched infinitely before him, the deep blue water sparkling under the sun, inviting him to uncover its secrets.

He dreamt of distant lands and the unique experiences that awaited him with every wave the *Esso-Frankfurt* would conquer. As he listened to the chatter of the crew and felt the rhythm of life aboard the ship, Lothar realised he was part of something larger than himself.

The sense of purpose and belonging filled his heart as each wave crashed against the hull, reminding him that this was only the beginning of a voyage filled with challenges, camaraderie, and the wondrous call of the sea.

As a mess boy on the ship, Lothar's duties encompassed a variety of tasks aimed at maintaining the well-being and morale of the crew. The role was essential in ensuring smooth operations during voyages, and Lothar approached it with a sense of responsibility and eagerness to learn.

He assisted the cook in preparing meals, which included chopping vegetables, cleaning seafood, and ensuring all ingredients were ready for cooking. Learning recipes and techniques from the seasoned chef was a rewarding aspect of his job.

Before mealtime, he arranged tables and laid out utensils, plates, and napkins in the mess area, creating a welcoming space for the crew to enjoy their meals together.

During meal service, Lothar helped serve food to crew members, ensuring that everyone received their portions in an efficient manner. He often enjoyed sharing stories and laughter with the crew during these moments.

After meals, Lothar was responsible for clearing tables, washing dishes, and maintaining cleanliness in the galley and mess area. He learned the importance of hygiene at sea, especially in ensuring that the kitchen remained organized and sanitary.

He assisted in keeping track of food supplies, helping to inform the cook when items were running low. This task taught him about resource management and the importance of planning for long voyages.

Beyond meal preparation, Lothar also helped with other tasks around the ship, which included mopping floors, taking out trash, and ensuring that kitchen equipment was in good condition,

Lothar learned the unwritten rules of life at sea, including respect for fellow crew members and the importance of teamwork. His position required him to be observant, understanding the dynamics of the crew and adapting to their needs.

He received training in safety protocols, ensuring he knew what to do in case of emergencies. Understanding fire safety in the kitchen, for example, was crucial.

Through these duties, Lothar developed invaluable skills, not only in cooking and cleanliness but also in teamwork, responsibility, and time management. Each day brought new challenges and lessons as he embraced his role as a mess boy on the *Esso-Frankfurt*, fostering connections with the crew and becoming a vital part of the ship's community.

On one tumultuous day as he was entering the Captain's Quarters to serve a bowl of soup to the captain, the rough sea twisted everything into chaos. Lothar dropped the bowl of soup and landed on top of it. In the mess hall, plates clattered; and food sloshed over the tables Lothar struggled to keep his footing, his stomach turning with each rise and fall of the ship.

Lothar's stomach churned in protest betraying his youthful inexperience in the face of the fierce elements. Unable to control the roiling sea within him, he stumbled to the railing and emptied the contents of his stomach into the unforgiving depths below, his face pale and strained with effort. "Working on a ship is not a holiday." Lothar whispered to himself.

After a week or so, tensions simmered between Lothar and the head steward and chef who accused Lothar of stealing food from the pantry. A simple disagreement over duties had spiralled into a heated argument, each word a jagged edge in the turbulent sea of emotions that threatened to engulf them both.

As the night wore on, Lothar found himself grappling with another challenge peculiar to his youth – the strict rule that required him to retire to bed early while the older crew members had to stayed up late, bonding over tales of voyages, songs and drinks.

This injustice burned within Lothar like a smouldering ember, igniting a fiery rebellion against the confines of tradition and hierarchy that sought to define his place on the ship. "Why should age dictate my worth?" he mused bitterly, the sense of injustice fuelling his resolve to defy the constraints imposed upon him. Overwhelmed by fear, nausea and the crew's unfriendly behaviour, Lothar decided to breach his contract after a few months.

After breaching his first contract as a sailor, Lothar returned to his hometown in Gelsenkirchen, feeling a mix of disappointment and regret. The familiar streets, once comforting, now felt confining; the echoes of his maritime dreams haunted him as he passed by old houses and familiar faces.

He spent his days wrestling with his thoughts, working odd jobs and reminiscing about the adrenaline of the open sea, the salty air, and the camaraderie of some of his fellow sailors. As weeks turned into months, the tug of the ocean grew stronger. The allure of the waves, the promise of adventure, and the chance to reclaim his place on a ship began to overshadow his initial fears and failures.

He envisioned himself navigating through storms, discovering distant shores, and finding purpose in the rhythm of life at sea. Driven by this newfound resolve, Lothar spent sleepless nights refining his skills and researching opportunities.

CHAPTER 4
FROM NAUTICAL DREAMS TO HOMEWARD BOUND

Lothar stepped off the train in Hamburg, the salty breeze curling around him like a familiar friend. Memories of his first adventure as a sailor flooded back – dreams of adventure and the open seas had drawn him in, but the chaos of his last experience had crushed those hopes. This time, he was determined to find his place among the sailors once again, ready to prove himself anew.

However, as he approached various shipping companies, hope quickly turned to despair. One by one, their hiring managers shook their heads, their expressions a mixture of sympathy and frustration. "You breached your first contract" they said, the words loaded with finality. "We can't risk hiring someone with your record." Lothar's stomach sank each time, the weight of his past mistakes anchoring him in place.

Frustrated and dismayed, Lothar stepped into a dimly lit bar in Hamburg, the hum of conversation blending with the clinking of glasses. He ordered a bottle of beer, its coldness a temporary balm for the frustration bubbling beneath his surface. As he sat at the counter, his mind swirled with thoughts of rejection and failed dreams.

A matured woman seated a few stools down caught his eye. Her presence was warm and grounded, an aura of understanding surrounding her. She observed him closely, sensing the heaviness in his demeanour. After a moment, she slid over and leaned against the bar beside him. "You look like the world's been a bit hard on you," she said, her voice inviting yet gentle.

Lothar sighed, his defences lowering slightly. "I'm just… just…trying to find my way back to the sea," he confessed, glancing down at the bottle before him. "I could not even buy you a drink. I am broke." Her gaze softened. "Sometimes, when the waves toss us around, it's easy to lose sight of where we want to go. But every storm passes, and it's what we learn in the stillness that guides us." Lothar looked at her, surprised by her insight. In that fleeting moment, he felt a connection, a reminder that beneath the struggles lay hope and the chance for a new beginning. As he took a sip of his beer, he realised she was right. Maybe the sea was still waiting for him, and with her steady presence, he felt the first stirrings of confidence to face whatever came next.

"You need a rest, young man. You can temporarily stay in my room but there is only a double bed, a cupboard, a table and a chair. If I come home with a guy, just roll to the other side and ignore us. Tomorrow, we will talk about the seafaring job." Lothar found solace at the prostitute's modest apartment. One evening as they shared stories over dinner, she revealed her past. "I was once a promising daughter of an influential family but was disinherited after having a child out of wedlock.

Her eyes held a mix of sadness and strength, a reflection of her difficult journey. "I forged my own path," she said, "but it hasn't been easy. Family can be both a blessing and a curse." Unbeknownst to Lothar, the woman's brother was a supervisor at a prominent shipping company.

THE LAST HORIZON

Learning about Lothar's aspirations to return to the sea, she made a few discreet phone calls. The very next day, Lothar was instructed to go to the Sailor's Registration Officer and look for a certain person. The guy took his details and gave Lothar a new sailor's book. In that moment, he understood that kindness, even from the most unexpected places and the most stigmatized of people, could chart a new course in life, guiding him back to the waves he longed to embrace, for the second time around.

It was on 11th April 1957 when Lothar signed the new contract with *World Toil* ship for the same position – a mess boy. The *World Toil* ship owned by the London Company Greek Niachos would go into the dock in Antwerp, Belgium for servicing and then would go on its voyage to Venezuela, South America. The contract shows he was hired to earn the following wages:

65.00 Deutschmark per month
3.75 Tanker ship extra
17.06 Foreign flag
8.00 Overtime per month
93.31 Deutschmark per month in total

This time he was to replace a new member in Antwerp, Belgium. Lothar stepped off the train in Antwerp, Belgium, the salty breeze from the nearby docks invigorating him as he made his way to the *World Toil* ship on the dry dock.

The vessel loomed majestically, but he felt a twinge of disappointment when he learned most of the sailors were on leave while the ship underwent servicing. Undeterred, he rolled up his sleeves and was assigned to work in the cool rooms, tasked with stocktaking and cleaning the kitchen.

MAGGIE CUDANIN EBBINGHAUS

The coolness inside was a relief from the warm Spring sun outside. As he organised crates of provisions and scrubbed down surfaces, Lothar felt a sense of purpose return. He listened to the rhythmic sounds of hammers and brushes as other workers painted and repaired the ship, their camaraderie evident in their shared laughter and banter.

Though his work was humble, each item he counted and every surface he polished felt like a step closer to the life he craved. Lothar found himself dreaming of the open sea while surrounded by metallic boxes of food and supplies, imagining the adventures ahead.

As the sun set over Antwerp, the sailors were buzzing with excitement, celebrating the end of a long week with a pub crawl through the lively streets. Lothar joined in, laughter echoing against the brick walls as frothy mugs of beer clinked and stories flowed. But as the evening wore on, he felt the warmth of the drink turn to heaviness, the chatter around him fading into a dull roar.

Overwhelmed, Lothar slipped away from the group, stepping onto the quiet street, the cool night air refreshing against his flushed skin. He wandered aimlessly, thoughts of home in Germany weighing heavily on his mind. The longing for familiarity and comfort tugged at him, urging him to return if only for the weekend. In a moment of impulsive clarity, he decided to hitch a ride back to Germany, planning to return to Antwerp the next working day. He stuck out his thumb, feeling a rush of hope as the first car stopped just 20 kilometres from the German border. The driver, a kind older man, smiled and dropped him off with friendly waves and encouraging words.

Feeling a renewed sense of determination, Lothar resumed his hitchhiking, this time catching the attention of a passing police car. The officers inside smiled knowingly as they recognised a traveller in need, waving him over. They spoke Flemish which Lothar had no idea about.

However, the police officers knew that Lothar was drunk, so they took him to the Police Station and locked him up in a cell with a straw-covered floor to sleep on. As morning broke, Lothar stood nervously before the German-speaking police officer scrutinising him with a mix of curiosity and amusement. "So, you hitchhiked all the way from Antwerp just to get home for breakfast?" the officer asked, a grin spreading across his face as Lothar recounted his impulsive journey and the nights spent longing for the comforts of home. "Have some breakfast before I escort you to the German border." The benevolent police officer offered him.

Upon reaching the border, Lothar was unceremoniously dropped off, the police officer's parting words echoing in his mind. With nothing but the clothes on his back, Lothar took a deep breath and started the next chapter of his journey – hitchhiking his way home. He ventured along the roadside, extending his thumb to passing vehicles, each car symbolising hope and the promise of a return to normalcy.

Hours passed as Lothar continued to hitchhike, the sun sinking lower and casting long shadows along the road. With each pickup, his anticipation grew, the rhythm of his heart quickening with every mile that brought him closer to Gelsenkirchen. Finally, as the golden hues of the afternoon began to wash over the landscape, he caught sight of his hometown's welcoming signs. Arriving in Gelsenkirchen felt surreal. Lothar hurried through the familiar streets, each turn evoking memories of his childhood, both joyous and bittersweet. As he reached the doorstep of his childhood home, he paused, taking a deep breath, overwhelmed by a mix of emotions.

At that moment, Lothar's mother opened the door, her eyes widening in disbelief. For a heartbeat, time seemed to stand still; then her face broke into a radiant smile that lit up the entire afternoon. She rushed forward, her arms outstretched, her joy infinite. Lothar felt a wave of warmth wash over him, as if the burdens of the past few days melted away with each step they shared towards each other.

In that embrace, Lothar knew he was finally home. His mother, the happiest creature on earth, held her son as if she were reclaiming a piece of her heart, and in that moment, all the struggles and trials seemed to fade into a distant memory.

As they gathered around the dinner table, bowls steaming with rich, hearty stew, stories flowed as freely as the laughter. Lothar felt a swelling in his chest, a sense of belonging that wrapped around him tighter than any hug. Each spoonful of Eintopf reminded him of all the flavours at home – comforting, familiar and filled with love.

The surreal sense of returning after such a whirlwind journey filled him with mixed emotions. He had dreamed of the sea, of adventure and freedom, yet the chaos of hitchhiking and the endless longing weighed heavily on his heart. What a homecoming it was! It was a stark contrast to the life at sea. He concluded that he was not meant to be a sailor.

Lothar's mother Else recognised Lothar's potential and the importance of pursuing a more fulfilling career in Gelsenkirchen. Working at the *Hans* Sacks Haus restaurant, Else had established connections in the local arts community and was keen to help her son find a position that aligned with his interests and skills.

When Else learned of an opening for a stage technician, she encouraged Lothar to apply. She understood that working in the theatre would not only allow him to utilise his hands – on abilities but also immerse him in the vibrant world of performance arts. Excited yet apprehensive, Lothar pursued this new opportunity, feeling a spark of passion ignited by the idea of being part of something more creative and dynamic.

Lothar quickly adapted to the challenges presented by his new job. Each performance was a collective effort and Lothar thrived on the excitement of working behind the curtain, contributing to the magic of the theatre.

Lothar's mother watched with pride as her son blossomed into his new role. She saw how he emerged from the challenges of his past work, eager to learn and grow in an environment that excited him. Her belief in him not only opened doors but also allowed Lothar to forge his own path, combining hard work with creativity in a fulfilling career.

Through this journey, Lothar stepped into a vibrant world of performance, illustrating how support, determination and opportunity can lead to personal and professional transformation.

CHAPTER 5
A NEW HORIZON
THE THRILL OF MIGRATION

In the 1950s, Australia was actively recruiting European migrant workers to help bolster its post-war economy and address a labour shortage. This initiative opened the door for many individuals seeking new opportunities far from their homelands. Among those captivated by this prospect was twenty year-old Lothar, whose curiosity and adventurous spirit began to stir as he learned about the possibilities in the distant land.

Lothar found himself increasingly intrigued by stories of Australia – the vast landscapes, vibrant cities, and promise of a fresh start. The thought of moving to a country so different from his own ignited a sense of excitement within him. He envisioned palm trees swaying in the breeze, sunny beaches, and the unique wildlife that Australia had to offer.

It was a world of adventure waiting to be explored. Lothar's yearning for adventure grew stronger as he considered the opportunities that lay ahead. He thought about the experiences he could gain, the people he would meet, and the chance to immerse himself in a culture that was both foreign and exhilarating.

He felt that going to a faraway country would not just be a physical journey, but an opportunity for personal growth and transformation. Motivated by this adventurous dream, Lothar began to research more about the migration process and the option available to him.

As he weighed the decision, Lothar began to reflect on what such a move would mean to his life. He considered the challenges – leaving behind his familiar surroundings, family and friends – as well the opportunities for new beginnings.

After making the bold decision to pursue a new life in Australia, Lothar took the necessary steps to apply for a working visa. He meticulously gathered all the required documents, filled out the application forms, and paid 250 Deutsche Marks. He submitted his request with a sense of both hope and anticipation. The waiting period that followed felt like an eternity, filled with moments of doubt and excitement as he envisioned what life would be like in a completely different country.

After a month filled with anxious anticipation, Lothar received the long-awaited news: his working visa for Australia had been granted. Overwhelmed with joy, he felt an exhilarating rush of emotions. This document symbolised not just permission to work; it was a ticket to adventure, opportunities and a fresh start in a land where he hoped to find his place.

With his visa in hand, Lothar knew it was time to say goodbye to his current position at the theatre Stattische Buenen. He valued the experiences and connections he had made there, yet he felt a strong pull toward his new path. Taking a deep breath, he sat down to write a resignation letter. He expressed his gratitude for the support and camaraderie he had experienced in the theatre, fondly recalling the moments spent behind the scenes and the friendships he had formed.

With the letter in hand, he approached his supervisor Albert, his heart racing yet filled with determination. As he handed over the letter, he explained his reasons for leaving and shared his excitement about the move to Australia.

His supervisor, while saddened to let him go, understood his desire for growth and adventure. He offered words of encouragement, wishing him all the best in his new life. Lothar invited all his friends and colleagues in the Green Room of the theatre for a farewell party.

As he prepared for his departure, Lothar reflected on the vibrant path ahead of him, eager to explore new possibilities and embrace the adventure that awaited him down under. With his visa secured and his farewell completed, he was one step closer to turning his dreams into reality.

However, amidst his jubilation, an unexpected letter arrived from the Ministry of Defence. Lothar unfolded the notice. It stated that he was required to conscript in the army. The letter cast a shadow over his elation and nervousness crept into his heart. Lothar found himself torn between two conflicting emotions – the thrill of a new beginning and the apprehension of mandatory military service. He pondered the choices before him, weighing his aspirations against his obligations to his country.

The thought of trading his aspirations for a rifle and uniform weighed heavily on his spirit. Lothar knew deep down that his goal lay beyond the borders of his Fatherland, in the sun-drenched shores of a land brimming with promise and potential.

Determined to find a way out of his predicament, Lothar sought counsel from his former boss in the city theatre (Stattische Buenen)- Albert Zotsman, a very influential personality and a wise and seasoned mentor who had always supported his ambitions.

He was the one who advised Lothar to delete the word 'impossible' from his vocabulary telling him that everything is possible. He concluded by sharing a famous saying from Napoleon HIll: "What your mind can conceive and believe, you will achieve." This wisdom kept reverberating in Lothar's mind. With a heavy heart and a sense of urgency, Lothar laid bare his dilemma, expressing his fears and hopes in equal measure.

Albert confidently said: "Go and pursue your Australian dream. After one week, I will give this notice to the authorized officer and will tell him that you were already on your journey to Australia when this notice arrived in the mail."

As Lothar prepared for his departure, he reflected on the vibrant path ahead of him, eager to explore new possibilities and embrace the adventure that awaited him. With his visa secured and his farewell completed, he was one step closer to turning his dreams into reality.

He took the train to Bremen 244 kilometres away from his residence in Gelsenkirchen, Westphalia on 13th March 1959, to board the Castel Felice– an old Italian-owned ship transporting migrants to Australia and New Zealand.

The Castel Felice In 1959
(photo from collections.museumsvictoria.com.au website)

As Lothar bade farewell to his Fatherland, his heart light with gratitude and determination, he knew that the road ahead would be fraught with challenges and uncertainties.

Lothar stood on the bustling dock of Bremen, his heart racing with excitement as he prepared to board the ship. The massive vessel loomed before him, its hull gleaming under the sun, ready to take him across the vast ocean to Australia Armed with the unwavering resolve of a dreamer chasing his destiny, Lothar boarded the *Castel Felice* to set sail towards the sun-drenched shores of Australia, where a new chapter of his life awaited, filled with promise, hope, and the infinite possibilities of a land brimming with opportunity.

Aboard the vessel were the Italian crew and hundreds of German migrants. Once on board, Lothar was drawn to the lively atmosphere of the ship. Passengers mingled, laughter echoed in the air, and the smell of fresh sea breeze filled his lungs.

As the ship set sail, it glided past the rugged coast of Portugal where cliffs kissed by crashing waves whispered tales of ancient mariners and voyages. Lothar soon crossed paths with two fellow passengers, Peter from Germany and Oscar from Hungary both of whom were also embarking on their own journeys to new beginnings.

The three quickly struck up a conversation, sharing their backgrounds and reasons for leaving their homelands. They discovered common ground in their dreams, aspirations and the thrill of starting anew. The ship's sway became the backdrop of their g rowing friendship as they exchanged stories about their lives from childhood memories to the challenges, they faced in making the decision to migrate.

Soon, the ship reached the famed Gibraltar Passage; a narrow strait flanked by the iconic Rock of Gibraltar which stood as a sentinel guarding the gateway between the Atlantic Ocean and the Mediterranean Sea. Lothar marvelled at the beauty of the coastline and its rocky shores crowned with picturesque villages bathed in the golden light of dawn. The water danced with the mesmerising flow of the currents, creating a sense of anticipation and awe among the passengers who lined the decks to witness the natural wonder.

THE LAST HORIZON

As the ship navigated the Passage with expert precision, Lothar's gaze wandered across the glistening waters, his thoughts drifting back to a time when he got his first job on the Esso-Frankfurt tanker ship as a mess boy. The Castel Felice cut through the azure waters of the Mediterranean Sea; its destination clear - Australia.

On this particular journey, the ship had an important stop to make in the picturesque island nation of Malta. As the *Castel Felice* docked in the Grand Harbour in Valletta, the capital city of Malta, a sense of anticipation and excitement filled the air.

On the quay stood a group of 800 Maltese men, women and children, their eyes alight with hope and dreams of a better future across the seas. They were also embarking on a journey that would take them far from their familiar shores to a distant land full of promise.

Families clutched their belongings tightly, their hearts heavy with the bittersweet emotions of leaving behind their homeland yet brimming with optimism for the adventure that lay ahead. Children ran about, their laughter mingling with the calls of the seagulls overhead, a scene of both farewell and new beginnings unfolding before their eyes.

As the days at sea passed, Lothar, Peter and Oscar formed a close bond. They shared meals in the dining hall, explored the ship's decks and even offered each other encouragement during the challenges of seasickness.

The trio spent evenings laughing under the starry skies, sharing dreams and making plans. They became a support system for one another, an instant family on this journey, each facing the unknown together.

The engines of the ship rumbled to life again as the Castel Felice resumed its journey across the vast expanse of the Mediterranean Sea. Lothar noticed that the ship was taking the route to the Suez Canal. He vividly remembered this route when he worked as a mess boy on the

Esso-Frankfurt tanker ship three years before.

As the salty sea breeze caressed his short curly hair, Lothar closed his eyes, allowing the memories of his time aboard the **Esso Frankfurt** to flood his mind. He could almost hear the creak of the ship's timbers, the roar of the engines and the laughter of his crewmates when he spit his guts out when the sea got rough.

He could almost feel his experience that fateful night as the sea grew restless and the wind howled like a banshee, when he was carrying a bowl of soup for the Captain and accidentally dropped it.

As the Castel Felice sliced through the tranquil waters of the Suez Canal, Lothar leaned against the railing, taking in the warm breeze and the vast expanse of the desert beyond. Lothar, Peter and Oscar spent long hours on deck swapping stories of their past.

Lothar stood at the railing of the majestic Castel Felice ship, feeling a cool breeze on his light-complexioned face as the vessel gracefully navigated the vast expanse of the

Indian Ocean. "As a passenger on this ship, I cherish every moment of freedom. This is a stark contrast to my previous experience aboard the Esso-Frankfurt where I worked as a mess boy." Lothar said to his new friends Peter and Oscar.

As he reflected on the journey, the Castel Felice had become more than just a mode of transformation – it was a vessel of transformation, carrying him towards a new chapter in his life. Operating as a vital link between Europe and Australia, she carried migrants from Bremen, Germany to the shores of their new homeland. Each trip was a significant undertaking, filled with the stories of individuals and families eager to embark on a fresh chapter in their lives.

CHAPTER 6
THE JOURNEY

The one-way voyage aboard *Castel Felice* took approximately six weeks, a journey marked by anticipation and uncertainty. As the ship set sail from the bustling port of Bremen, its hull cut through the waters of the North Sea, leaving behind the familiar landscapes of Europe. Passengers gazed back wistfully at their homeland, filled with memories, while looking ahead to the vast unknown that awaited them.

Life on board was a mix of camaraderie and introspection. Migrants shared their hopes and fears, swapping stories of their past lives and discussing the dreams they held for their future in Australia. For many, this voyage was their first long journey at sea, and while it was invigorating, it also presented challenges. The close quarters and confined environment sometimes led to feelings of homesickness and nostalgia.

Days were filled with activities designed to pass time. Lothar was intrigued by the prospect of attending English classes offered on board. However, to his relief, he was assessed to have possessed the basic English conversational skills. He was superb in Mathematics, too, thanks to the rigorous education system in Germany when he was young.

When he had to bid farewell to his school and embark on new adventures after six years, he couldn't help but feel a sense of gratitude for the valuable lesson – that perseverance, discipline and hard work were the cornerstone of success in any endeavour.

Passengers would gather for meals in the dining areas, often sharing laughter and building friendships. Others might take to the deck, watching the waves roll by; their minds racing with thoughts of the opportunities that awaited them.

Lothar, among the crowd, would find solace in these moments, reminiscing about both his journey as a migrant and his unforgettable experience about his first kiss while his new friends Peter and Oscar listened to his story. "I remember my first kiss when I was twelve, I met a very attractive girl guide and we were both infatuated with each other. We arranged a date in one of the corner streets.

My stepfather would not allow me to go out at night, so I had to wait until I heard him snoring before I sneaked through the back door." Lothar continued. "I found Clara on a quiet corner street illuminated by a flickering lantern. Her eyes sparkled in the dim light as we talked and talked about everything and nothing, our words floating into the night like delicate wisps of smoke. As our conversation grew more animated, I felt a rush of emotions I had never experienced before.

In a bold moment of impulse, I leaned in and planted a gentle kiss on Clara's cheek, my heart pounding in my chest like a wild drum. But as soon as my lips touched her skin, a wave of panic overwhelmed me - *maybe my father had woken up and noticed that I was not in my bedroom and maybe he realised that I sneaked out through the back door* - was going on in my mind. I ran as fast as my legs could carry me, leaving Clara standing there. I fled from Clara that night, and never saw her again, but the memory of our fleeting encounter stayed with me." Lothar recalled.

As the ship moved on Lothar, Peter and Oscar continued to share experiences that impacted their lives.

As *Castel Felice* approached the shores of Australia after her six weeks voyage. Excitement and nervousness filled the air. The sight of distant land represented more than just a new country, it signified the culmination of dreams, ambitions and the beginning of an entirely new chapter for each migrant aboard the *Castel Felice*. In these final moments of the journey, Lothar and his fellow travellers felt a mixture of anticipation and gratitude for the voyage they had shared – one that would forever shape their lives.

On a cool autumn 5th May 1959, the *Castel Felice* glided into the inactive port of Fremantle, Western Australia. With a heart full of dreams and a spirit renewed, Lothar looked out and saw some flickering lights from a distance. "We must experience our first night life in Australia." Lothar suggested. They were filled with excitement as they stepped onto the streets of Fremantle quickly hailing a taxi to set off into the heart of the city of Perth.

As the taxi wound its way through the bustling streets, Lothar, Peter and Oscar gazed out at the glittering lights in Perth, anticipation building with each passing moment. Their imaginations ran wild with visions of trendy nightclubs, cosy bars and bustling streets filled with revellers enjoying the night. However, their excitement soon turned into confusion as they discovered a surprising truth upon arriving in the city – all the nightclubs and bars closed at 6 p.m.

The trio exchanged bewildered glances, unable to comprehend the early closing time that seemed to defy their expectations of a vibrant nightlife scene. Determined not to let this setback dampen their spirits, Lothar, Peter and Oscar decided to wander the quiet street. They stood resplendent in their European attire, exuding an air of sophistication and style that turned heads as they loitered in front of a movie theatre in the heart of Perth. Dressed in polished shoes, Stetson hats and slim ties, the trio cut a striking figure against the backdrop of the marquee lights and throngs of passersby.

As they chatted and laughed amongst themselves, the attention of a passing couple was caught by the impeccable appearance of the three guys. They had never seen Australians wearing that kind of attire. The couple exchanged curious glances, their eyes widening with wonder at the sight of these dapperly dressed men who seemed to have stepped out of a bygone era.

At that moment, an idea sparked in the couple's minds. "Are you actors from that movie?" they asked Lothar, Oscar and Peter. With a nod and smile, they embraced the roles that had been unwittingly thrust upon them. "I told you so!" the wife said to her husband.

As the couple moved on with smiles of delight and admiration, the trio shared a secret grin, hailed a taxi and went back to the ship that would take them to their final destination – Melbourne Australia. As the weary migrants disembarked, a sense of anticipation filled the air.   For many, long lost European relatives eagerly awaited their arrival, their faces etched with both joy and relief.

Amidst the chaotic scene at the harbor, families tearfully reunited, embracing each other tightly after years of separation. Laughter and tears mingled in a mix of emotions as loved ones shared stories and caught up on lost time. The air buzzed with German, Italian, Maltese and other European languages, a cacophony of accents blending into a tapestry of human connection.

However, not everyone had someone waiting for them at the port. For those migrants without relatives present, a different fate awaited them. They were ushered onto a train bound for Bonegilla, a migrant reception in Northeast Victoria. As the train chugged along, the landscape transformed from the bustling city to the rolling hills and wide-open spaces, a stark contrast to the cramped confines of the ship they had just left behind.

At Bonegilla Nissen Huts, these migrants found themselves in a new world, a temporary home where they would receive support and guidance as they began their new lives in Australia. Services and support offered to European migrants during that time included:

Meals – catering to the dietary needs of different migrant groups; Medical Services – basic healthcare;
English Language classes; Employment Assistance;
Cultural Orientation – to help migrants adapt to Australian customs, laws and way of life; Legal Assistance – to assist migrants with issues like visa applications, residency status and other legal matters.

Bonegilla played a crucial role in assisting European migrants like Lothar with their settlement process in Australia. As a curious and friendly character, Lothar formed an unlikely bond with three Italian migrants who were sent to Queensland to work in the sugarcane fields. He felt a deep longing to join his friends on their journey, to experience the freedom and challenges of life on the sugar plantation. However, fate had other plans for Lothar. The Bonegilla authorities, in their wisdom, had decided to send him to the Nullarbor Plains in Western Australia to work in railway construction.

Lothar sat in his Nissen hut at Bonegilla, his heart heavy with the prospect of being sent to work in the desolate Nullarbor. The thought of the vast, empty plains stretching endlessly before him filled him with dread.

After a restless night filled with conflicting thoughts, Lothar reflected on his options. He weighed the opportunity for steady work against his desire for freedom and exploration. Deep down, he knew he needed to take charge of his path. The thought of spending an indeterminate amount of time in a desolate region gnawed at him, and he felt an urge to forge his own way toward the city that had captured his imagination.

Fuelled by a quiet resolve, Lothar made a bold decision. He began to pack his belongings into a small travel bag. With 46 Australian Pounds in his pocket – his savings from his job in Germany – he made his way to the highway, determined to hitchhike his way to Melbourne where he hoped to start a life his way. Standing by the roadside, Lothar's heart raced with a mix of excitement and nervousness. Each passing car brought a surge of hope that someone would offer him a ride towards his destination.

Hours passed, the sun sinking lower in the sky, casting long shadows across the road. Finally, a kind soul in a weathered car pulled over, offering Lothar a ride. Grateful for the chance to move closer to his dreams, Lothar climbed in, the wind rushing through his blond hair as they sped down the Hume Highway towards Melbourne.

After finding shared accommodation in a cosy neighbourhood, he wasted no time in seeking employment to sustain his new beginning. As Lothar navigated through the bustling streets of Melbourne, he noticed a recurring theme among the various banks and businesses lining the thoroughfare. Bold advertisements plastered on their windows proclaimed, "Job Opening" and "Hiring Labourers," alongside listings for skilled positions as well. The promise of work felt like a beacon of hope to him, as he was eager to find a way to support himself after his recent arrival.

Inspired by the opportunities, Lothar decided to act. He stepped into one of the nearby banks, his determination heightening with each step. The interior was bright and filled with the sounds of murmuring clients. Approaching the reception desk, he politely inquired about the job openings that caught his eye. The tall receptionist advised him to head to the railway lane construction site the following morning. "They're in urgent need of labourers," the receptionist said.

Being 20 years old, Lothar was poised at a pivotal moment in his life, stepping into the realm of work and responsibility. Now employed at the Railway Lane construction site, he quickly learned that his age would influence his earnings. Each week, Lothar would take home ten (10)pounds while the twenty-one year-old labourers would earn eighteen (18)pounds a week. "I am only five months away from being twenty-one and I want to earn the full wage." Lothar insisted. "Go get some ink remover from the stationary shop and bring it to me," the recruiter instructed Lothar. With the ink remover, the recruiter altered Lothar's birth date to falsely present Lothar as twenty-one years old.

With his pick and shovel in hand, Lothar secured a job working in the challenging world of railway lane construction. The Italian foreman from Calabria deployed him to work with more than 100 Italians. From dawn until dusk, and sometimes well into the night, he worked tirelessly, shaping the earth and laying the foundations that would connect distant cities and towns.

Lothar's days blurred into each other as he poured his sweat and dedication into his work, clocking in an astonishing 80 hours a week including weekends. Saturdays and Sundays became no different from any other day for Lothar as he toiled under the sun or beneath the glow of flickering streetlights, driven by a quiet determination to succeed.

Amid his arduous routine, fate intervened in a surprising twist of serendipity. One day, while taking a brief respite from his labour, Lothar heard familiar voices calling up to him. Turning around, he saw two figures approaching – Oscar and Peter, the friends he made on the Castel Felice ship that had carried them to Australia. Reunited with his friends, a spark of joy ignited in Lothar's eyes.

The trio embraced warmly. While progress hung in the air and the promise of new beginnings beckoned to those willing to seize it, Lothar stood as a testament to the resilience and determination of the human spirit.

Amidst the landscape where labourers toiled for a modest wage of eighteen pounds a week, Lothar defied the odds with his unwavering work ethic and commitment to excellence. Working gruelling hours with unwavering dedication, he earned a remarkable forty pounds a week – a wage that set him apart from his peers and highlighted his exceptional work ethic. But wait! Lothar's exceptional work ethic seemed to give his foreman a problem. "I've noticed how fast you work." Lothar's foreman said to him over a cup of tea one cold winter morning. "While your efficiency is commendable, it has unintended consequences. When the supervisor sees you working at such a pace, he will expect the others to keep up with you. It puts undue pressure on the rest of the team."

A heavy silence hung between them punctuated only by the sizzling of the fire beneath the boiling kettle of tea. "I'm left with a difficult choice Lothar," the foreman continued, his gaze unwavering. "Either you slow down your pace to match the others, or I'm afraid I have to ask you for resignation." The weight of the foreman's ultimatum settled upon Lothar. With a heavy heart, he swiftly replied: "I want to keep my job, so I will work slower."

After a couple of months, Lothar found himself working as a painter of breweries and factories. The vibrant hues of paint and the scent of fresh varnish mingled in the air as he wielded his brush with expert precision, bringing life and colour to the industrial landscape that surrounded him.

Despite the physical distance that separated Lothar from his parents in Germany, he sought solace in the act of writing letters to them, penning his thoughts and experiences on weathered sheets of paper that bore the imprint of his journey. With each stroke of the pen, he poured out his heart, sharing tales of his new job, the people he met, and the sights and sounds of his adopted home.

Days turned into weeks, and weeks turned into months as the letters made their slow voyage across the vast expanse of land and sea, bridging the gap between Lothar and his loved ones with each passing mile. It took two long months for the missives to arrive in Gelsenkirchen where his parents awaited news of their son, their hearts yearning for his familiar presence and the charisma of his baritone voice every time he sang songs from the Opera.

As the letters finally reached their destination, bearing the imprint of distant lands and far-off adventures, a wave of homesickness washed over Lothar, enveloping him in a bittersweet embrace. The memories of his mother, his childhood, the familiar sights and sounds of his Fatherland, beckoned to him with a siren call, tugging at his heartstrings and stirring a longing that he had not fully realised until that moment.

Lothar sat quietly in his rented room in Melbourne, surrounded by the unfamiliarity of his new surroundings. The walls, with few personal touches, felt impersonal and cold, amplifying the solitude he had tried to escape. Suddenly, an overwhelming wave of homesickness washed over him, flooding his mind with memories of home in Germany.

Images of his mother filled his thoughts, her laughter, her gentle voice and the comforting aromas that wafted in the kitchen as she prepared his favourite meals. He could almost taste the rich flavours of her traditional dishes like *eintopf* which had always brought warmth to their family gatherings. He missed his brother Wolfgang and his stepfather Bill too.

As he reminisced, Lothar's heart ached for the companionship of his friends, the inside jokes, and the shared adventures that seemed distant now. He missed the familiar streets of his hometown, the laughter echoing in the air, and the comforting presence of his grandparents, where wisdom and kindness had shaped his childhood.

The realisation struck him deeply. Melbourne with all its opportunities, felt like an island, isolating him from the warmth of his past. In that moment of longing, Lothar understood that while he was on a journey of growth and exploration, he essence of home – filled with love, laughter and cherished memories – remained a vital part of who he was.

Feeling a renewed sense of longing for connection, Lothar decided to venture out and seek warmth in the company of others who shared his European roots. He had heard about the Austrian Club in St. Kilda, a gathering place where fellow migrants from his homeland came together to celebrate their culture and forge bonds in the foreign country.

With a mix of excitement and nervousness, Lothar arrived at the club. The sounds of lively conversation and laughter greeted him in an embrace of familiarity. The décor was reminiscent of cosy gatherings back in Germany, with wooden beams, rustic décor, and the vibrant colours of Austrian flags creating a sense of belonging. As he mingled among the crowd, Lothar soon found himself immersed in a conversation with his two friends Peter and Oscar who he had met on the ship.

Lothar felt an exhilarating rush as he reunited with his friends. Their camaraderie brought a familiar warmth, lifting his spirits after feelings of homesickness. Over soft drinks, the trio animatedly discussed their shared dreams, aspirations and adventures of an epic scale. Those were the days when Coca Cola was the only beverage served in pubs.

It was Peter who first proposed the grand idea, his eyes sparkling with enthusiasm. "What if we each bought a motorbike and rode from Melbourne back to Europe?" he said, his voice brimming with excitement. Oscar leaned forward, equally intrigued, suggesting the possible route. "We could ride to Darwin, then ship our bikes to Singapore, and from there, find a way to transport them to Europe."

The notion electrified Lothar. This was more than just a journey; it was a chance to embrace freedom, explore distant lands, and reconnect with their roots. The three friends began mapping out their adventure, pouring over maps while discussing the varying landscape they would traverse from the arid expanse of the Australian outback to the lush greenery of Southeast Asia.

They envisioned the thrill of the open road, the wind in their hair as they conquered winding roads and picturesque vistas. Every stop would be an opportunity to indulge in local cultures, meet new people, and create a wealth of memories to cherish.

Drinks flowed freely as dreams of exploration simmered in the eyes of the European migrants. Among them, a spirited French migrant shared his audacious plan – to trek along the 2,800-kilometre railway that traversed the vast Nullarbor Plains, embracing the rugged beauty of the outback in each step.

Meanwhile, a jovial group of Italians whispered animatedly in a corner, plotting a daring voyage around the perimeter of Australia on a homemade raft. Their laughter filled the air as they imagined the thrill of sailing the turquoise waters, discovering hidden coves and pristine beaches. Not far away, a pair of friends from Holland enthusiastically debated their own ambitious scheme – to cycle around the entirety of Australia, immersing themselves in the diverse landscapes and vibrant culture of the vast continent.

However, amid the chatter and excitement, a sobering truth lingered unnoticed – a lack of awareness about the scale and dangers of the Australian wilderness. The group did not fully grasp the enormity of the land they sought to conquer, nor the perils that awaited them.

Unbeknownst to them, Australia's rugged terrain was home to unforgiving creatures, from stealthy crocodiles lurking in murky waters to venomous insects and snakes that slithered unseen through the undergrowth.

The vastness of the outback held untold challenges, testing the mettle of even the most intrepid travellers. As the night wore on and the stars twinkled overhead, the migrants continued to revel in their grand plans, their hearts full of wonder and anticipation.

An ambitious goal took shape before the eyes of Lothar, Peter and Oscar - a tapestry of winding roads and breathtaking vistas, of shared laughter and unspoken understanding. Each detail of their journey was meticulously planned and eagerly anticipated.

As the day of their planned departure came close, Lothar, Oscar and Peter stood on the threshold of the grand adventure, their hearts ablaze with the promise of freedom and the allure of the open road. They believed that no distance was too great, no obstacle was too daunting.

As the sun rose over the sprawling expanse of the Australian Outback, Lothar, Oscar and Peter revved their motorbikes, their hearts brimming with anticipation at the prospect of their grand journey back to Europe.

Their quest to see Mt. Kosciuszko, the highest peak in Australia, stood as the first chapter of their adventure. Then, they would travel north right through the centre of Australia and on to the Northern Territory. In Darwin, they would travel on a ship to Singapore and take other ships in Southeast Asia that would take them to Europe.

CHAPTER 7
STAYING FOR LOVE: A CHANGE OF HEART

Before embarking on their odyssey, the trio made a detour to visit their dear friend Holdy's house, a quaint cottage nestled amidst the eucalyptus trees, where the promise of a heartfelt farewell awaited them. To their surprise, they found the house abuzz with visitors – Helga and Erika, two enchanting women whose presence cast a spell of beauty and grace over the gathering.

As Lothar's gaze met Helga's deep azure eyes, a spark ignited within him, a flame of longing and desire that threatened to consume his resolve and redirect his path. The challenges ahead were daunting, but they would face them with courage and determination, knowing that they carried with them hopes and dreams of a better future for themselves and their families.

Across the room, Peter was equally entranced by Erika's radiant smile and gentle spirit, finding himself drawn to her magnetic presence with a force he had not known before.

In the fleeting moments that followed, the seeds of love were sown, intertwining the fates of Lothar, Peter, Helga and Erika in an intricate dance of destiny. As the day wore on and the hours slipped away like grains of sand through an hourglass, a silent understanding passed between the newfound pairs, an unspoken agreement that bound them together in a web of emotions too powerful to resist.

With hearts full of newfound affection, Lothar and Peter made a decision that would alter the course of their journey. They chose to forego their original plan to return to Europe on their bikes, opting instead to stay behind with Helga and Erika, their souls entwined in a tapestry of blossoming love and unforeseen connections.

As the engine of their bikes fell silent and the road ahead faded into the distance, Oscar bid his friends a bittersweet farewell, his eyes reflecting a mixture of understanding and acceptance. With a heavy heart, he boarded a plane bound for Hungary, leaving behind the echoes of a journey that had taken an unexpected turn, forever altering the lives of those who had embarked upon it. And so, amidst the whisper of the wind and the laughter of newfound love, Peter married Erika and Lothar married Helga.

Helga was a talented award-winning hairdresser whose salon was a beacon of beauty and elegance in the bustling village square in Glenelg. Her skill with scissors and her eye for style earned her a loyal clientele and the admiration of all who crossed her path, but it was her gentle demeanour and infectious laughter that captured Lothar's heart from the very first moment they met.

Lothar's move to South Australia marked the beginning of a new chapter in his life. Initially, Lothar struggled to find a job. The local job market was competitive, and his previous experiences didn't seem to align with the opportunities available. Rather than feeling discouraged, Lothar decided to immerse himself in a new venture – he would learn hairdressing.

Inspired by Helga's dedication and the vibrant atmosphere of her salon, he spent hours observing her at work. As Lothar honed his skills, he transitioned from a novice to an integral part of the salon. He took on responsibilities such as washing women's hair, where he learned not just the technical aspects but also the importance of building relationships with clients.

Eager to further his education and refine his craft, Lothar dreamed of expanding his skills through advanced training. He set his sights on Paris, the epicentre of fashion and beauty, where he could learn cutting-edge hairdressing and techniques. With Helga's support, he applied to a prestigious program offered by L'Oreal.

Learning from master stylists, he absorbed invaluable techniques, trends and the philosophy behind hairdressing that transcended traditional boundaries. Upon returning to Australia, Lothar brought not only enhanced skills but also fresh perspectives that he shared with the salon's clientele.

As Lothar settled comfortably into his role at the salon and his hairdressing skills flourished, he found himself increasingly passionate about the tools of the trade. Eager to provide the best service possible, he realized that the quality of hairdressing tools could significantly impact the artistry of his craft.

With Germany's reputation for manufacturing precision tools, Lothar decided to import high-quality hairdressing equipment specifically professional hair dryers and Tondeo knives. When they arrived in the customs office, Lothar came to collect them. However, the hairdressing tools did not indicate their origin.

Lothar sat in the bustling customs office, surrounded by the clatter of paperwork and the occasional murmur of conversations. Before him lay a daunting task: 1000 hairdressing tools, each devoid of their origin. The customs officer had been stringent; without proper labelling, these tools would remain in a limbo, held up by the bureaucratic protocols.

With a deep breath, Lothar rolled up his sleeves and began his laborious task. He had been instructed to affix "Made in Germany" labels onto each item, a requirement designed to ensure compliance with shipping regulations. The sheer volume of tools was overwhelming.

As he started, Lothar set up an assembly line He picked each item, inspected it for quality and then carefully affixed the label. The repetitive motion soon created a rhythm, although his hands began to tire. He pushed through the fatigue knowing that each label represented not just compliance but also the quality and craftsmanship of German hairdressing tools.

As the sun dipped low and shadows stretched across the office floor, he affixed the last label. With all 1000 items now properly labelled, he presented them to the customs officer for inspection. The officer nodded in approval, and Lothar felt a wave of satisfaction. Despite the arduous day and the monotonous task, he knew his efforts would ensure these tools would find their way into the hands of skilled professionals, ready to make their mark in the world of hairdressing in Adelaide.

While hairdressing was something he enjoyed, deep inside Lothar's heart, he wanted to venture into something else that he could not explain. On a crisp autumn morning in Adelaide, his life took an unexpected turn as he crossed paths with a real estate agent whose charisma and passion for property ignited a spark within Lothar's soul. As they chatted about the nuances of the housing market and the thrill of matching clients with their dream homes, like a moth to a flame, Lothar found himself drawn to the world of real estate.

Inspired by the agent's enthusiasm and armed with a newfound sense of purpose, Lothar made the bold decision to venture into the realm of real estate himself. He immersed himself in the intricacies of the industry, studying market trends, attending seminars and honing his negotiation skills with unwavering determination. He became adept at spotting undervalued properties, seeing what others couldn't – a cracked façade might just need a coat of paint.

With unwavering determination, Lothar embarked on his first real estate transaction, a modest house that caught his eye with its charm and potential. Guided by his instincts and newfound knowledge, he navigated the complexities of buying and selling with a steady hand and a keen eye for detail.

While the tradespeople toiled tirelessly to revitalize the interiors and exteriors of the house, Lothar turned his attention to the neglected garden that surrounded the property like a forgotten treasure waiting to be unearthed. He decided to tend the overgrown bushes.

As he set them ablaze, he watched with satisfaction as the flames danced and crackled, unaware of the danger that lurked beneath the surface of his seemingly innocent task. Before he knew it, the fire spiralled out control, fuelled by the dry bushland and fanned by the gentle morning breeze, spreading rapidly towards the house. Upon smelling the smoke, the neighbours sprang into action, rallying together as a force of unity and determination. Armed with buckets of water, hoses and sheer grit, they fought valiantly to contain the inferno, their shouts and cries mingling with the roar of the flames in a cacophony of chaos and courage.

Through sweat and tears, they battled the blaze with unwavering resolve. As the last embers smouldered and the tendrils of smoke vanished into the sky, collective sigh of relief washed over the group as they were able to save the property that meant a lot to Lothar. After fully renovating the property and earning a few dollars, he started looking for another business adventure.

Lothar's adventurous spirit was a force of nature, propelling him into the dazzling and enigmatic world of Australian opals. Enchanted by the vibrant colours and unique patterns of these gemstones, he saw not just rocks but a canvas of nature's artistry waiting to be shared with the world. With an entrepreneurial mindset and a keen eye for beauty, Lothar made a bold decision to set up a business selling singlet opals in Los Angeles. Arriving from Australia, he stood at the bustling LA Airport, his suitcase packed to the brim with vibrant opal jewellery that sparkled under the fluorescent lights. The thrill of opportunity coursed through him; he had secured a grant from the Australian Trade Commission to introduce his beloved Australian opals to the American market thinking there were no opals in America.

Triplet opal jewellery features stunning gemstones made from three layers: a thin slice of opal, a backing (often made of black onyx or another material), and a protective top layer of clear quartz or glass. This construction enhances the opal's vibrant colours and patterns while providing durability. The mesmerising play of colour seen in triplet opals makes them a popular choice for unique and eye-catching jewellery pieces, from earrings to pendants. Ideal for both everyday wear and special occasions, triplet opal jewellery adds a touch of elegance and individuality to any ensemble.

The Australian Trade Commissioner in Los Angeles, California gave him the address of the Gemmological Institute of America (GIA). While GIA focuses on gem education, research and grading, it is also a prominent location where suppliers, dealers and enthusiasts gather for various gem-related activities. There were numerous jewellers and gemstone retailers in the vicinity of Wilshire Boulevard that specialised in opals and other gemstones.

After going through strict security protocols to enter the building, Lothar proudly presented his triplet opals to the jewellers. In return, they showed Lothar their singlet opal jewellery that featured a single, solid piece of opal without any layers or additional materials.

This type of opal is prized for its vibrant colours and unique patterns, which are the result of natural formation processes. Singlet opals are typically cut and polished into various shapes like big Indian heads and sailing boats. Each singlet opal reveals a one-of-a-kind appearance, making it a popular choice for those seeking distinctive and elegant pieces. The natural beauty of singlet opal jewellery is celebrated for its ability to capture light and display dynamic colour play, adding a touch of sophistication to any outfit.

Lothar felt a wave of insecurity after admiring the stunning singlet opal pieces on display. Their intricate beauty made his own triplet opal jewellery seem less desirable in comparison, leaving him feeling embarrassed and out of place. Disheartened by the thought that his product might not finda market in Los Angeles, he quickly packed his suitcase, determining that it was time to leave the city that had unveiled his insecurities rather than his artistry.

Still resolute and hopeful, Lothar returned to Australia with a renewed sense of purpose. He began exploring new opportunities. A new opportunity unfolded when he met Elio, a truck driver whose tales of an interstate transport business and the vastness of Australia captured his imagination. A spark of curiosity ignited within him. Elio was a man of few words, yet his stories painted vivid pictures of the open road, of endless stretches of asphalt disappearing into the horizon, of landscape that shifted and changed with each passing mile.

As he spoke of the cities and towns he crisscrossed in his rig, of the people he met and the sights he beheld, Lothar felt a yearning stir within him – a desire to earn money and to experience and explore beyond the familiar confines of his world. Intrigued by Elio's tales, Lothar found himself drawn to the life of a truck driver, to the allure of the open road and the freedom of the highway. He peppered Elio with questions, eager to learn more about the intricacies of interstate transport, the challenges of long- haul driving, and the wonders that awaited those who traversed the vast expanse of the Australian outback.

Elio spoke of the dual nature of truck driving – its allure and its challenges, its rewards and its risks. He regaled Lothar with tales of long, lonely stretches of highway, of perilous mountain passes and unforgiving weather, of the ever-present spectre of fatigue and danger that haunted every mile on the road.

With a tone both cautionary and compelling, Elio detailed the risks involved in truck driving – the constant vigilance to navigate treacherous terrain, the uncertainty of weather and road conditions, the ever-present threat of accidents and breakdowns. He spoke of the solitude that enveloped a driver like a shroud, the long hours spent alone with nothing but the hum of the engine.

And then there were the financial realities of the profession, the inconsistent income, the fluctuating demand for transport services, the volatile nature of the industry that could see fortunes rise and fall with the shifting winds of supply and demand. Elio laid bare the harsh truths of life on the road, the sacrifices and compromises that came with the territory, the toll that the relentless grind could exact on the mind, body, and spirit. But despite the warnings, despite the tales of hardship and uncertainty, Lothar felt a flicker of determination ignite within him; a stubborn spark of courage and curiosity that refused to be quenched.

With a steely glint in his eye, Lothar gave a nod of resolve and decided to take a chance, to embrace the unknown, to venture into the world of truck driving with the spirit of adventure and a heart full of hope. He knew the road ahead would be fraught with obstacles yet he knew that within those challenges lay the promise of growth, of discovery, of a life unbounded by the confines of the familiar.

Lothar stood before the sprawling, sunburnt landscape of Australia, a long way from his childhood in Germany. The thrill of becoming a truck driver pulsed through him like the engine of the rig he was set to master. With a weathered road map in one hand and a thick rulebook in the other, he dove into preparation. Days turned into weeks as he memorised routes that twisted through the Outback, studied speed limits, and committed safety protocols to heart. The road was unforgiving, with wide expanses dotted with roadhouses and trucks laden with dreams of distant destinations.

Finally, the day arrived. Lothar clutched his newly upgraded driver's license tightly as he climbed into the cab of a vintage International. The hum of the engine echoed his excitement. With a smile, he shifted the gear, letting the open road wrap around him like a warm embrace. As he drove into the horizon, Lothar felt a sense of freedom. This was the beginning of many long hauls, each one filled with adventure, the promise of new friendships, and the unwavering rhythm of the road beneath him.

Lothar's hands gripped the steering wheel tightly as he navigated the bitumen roads of Australia. As a novice truck driver, he focused intently on the rhythm of the engine and the flow of the traffic in Parramatta, one of the busiest suburbs of Sydney. He stopped at the red light, the bright sun beating down on the cab. He shifted nervously, glancing at the other drivers impatiently tapping their steering wheels. Finally, the light turned green. Taking a deep breath, he released the clutch and pressed the accelerator expecting to surge forward. Instead, the truck rolled backward. Ice-cold fear gripped him as he turned his head to see the annoyed faces of the drivers behind him, furious horns blaring like angry lions. Panic rose in his chest as he fumbled with the controls, but the truck refused to cooperate.

Just as the weight of embarrassment threatened to crush him, a friendly face appeared in his mirror. A driver from behind had jumped out of his vehicle and hurried over with a reassuring smile. "Hey there mate! Looks like you could use some help." Lothar nodded grateful yet flustered. He requested the man to take the wooden wedge near the fuel tank and place it under the drive wheel so he could release the brakes and contact the mechanic.

The helpful driver offered his shortwave radio and contacted the mechanic while Lothar swallowed his frustration. Lothar stood beside his truck, anxiety knotting his stomach. It was his first week as a truck driver, and the vehicle refused to start. The sun was setting, casting long shadows, and he felt the weight of his inexperience pressing down on him. Just then the mechanic arrived, his toolbox in hand. After a quick inspection under the truck, he stood up, wiping grease from his hands onto the rag. "It's a broken axle," he said, noticing Lothar's puzzled expression. "Axle? What's that?" Lothar's voice trembled.

The mechanic chuckled softly, sensing Lothar's nervousness. "It's the part that helps the wheels turn smoothly and you have one spare axle under your truck. Don't worry, I'll take care of it." With efficient movements, the mechanic set to work, replacing the broken part with skill and confidence.

Within the hour the truck roared back to life, and Lothar's nervousness faded into relief. "Thanks a lot! I didn't even know what an axle was!" he exclaimed. The mechanic smiled, dusting off his hands. "That's why I'm here. Just remember, every driver starts somewhere. You'll get the hang of it."

Lothar got the hang of driving. Through experience, he learned to become half a mechanic too. He became friends with other long-haul truck drivers like Kurt Jackel a German migrant, Vince dele Tosso originally from Italy and Jo Dionisio from Austria. They often drove next to each other, the sprawling outback offering a unique blend of challenges and freedom.

However, it was during one fateful journey that he faced one of his greatest trials: getting bogged in a muddy outback road. The backdrop of the

Australian outback is mesmerising, with its red earth, scattered shrubs, and the endless stretch of the horizon. As Lothar navigated the remote routes, he felt the thrill of exhilaration and purpose, delivering essential goods to communities and mining sites far removed from urban conveniences.

One afternoon, however, the weather took a turn, and rain cascaded down, transforming the dusty road into a treacherous muddy path. While driving along one particularly remote stretch of road, Lothar suddenly felt his truck sink into the mud. The wheels spun helplessly, losing traction with each attempt to inch forward. Panic set in as he realised he was well off the beaten path, far the nearest town or help.

Those were the days when telephone booths could only be found in the big towns. Stranded and surrounded by an unforgiving landscape, thoughts of unease crept into his mind. Just when despair threatened to overwhelm him, another truck driver Kurt, informed him about the group of American iron mining specialists operating nearby in Western Australia.

Gathering his courage he decided to reach out for help using the one-way radio of his friend's truck. After explaining his predicament, the Americans quickly responded. With a can-do attitude, they sprang into action employing their machinery and expertise to free Lothar's truck from the muddy grip of the road. The experience not only taught Lothar an invaluable lesson about the unpredictability of working in the outback but also emphasised the importance of community and support.

Lothar hauled all sorts of freight including 800 prefabricated houses for the mining camps in Western Australia. He delivered all sorts of goods like vegetables and fruits, iron ore, and general freight. From Albany in south Western Australia, he delivered a seed-cleaning machine to a farm in Mareeba, Far North Queensland. He navigated a gruelling 9,000 kilometres of corrugated dirt road over the course of three weeks a journey that tested both his endurance and determination.

The bumpy terrain jostled his 100-horsepower truck relentlessly, leaving him fatigued and weary by the end of each day. Dust coated everything, and the isolation of the outback was both breathtaking and daunting.

The sight of litter along roads and highways was an issue way back then. Drivers often carelessly discarded all manner of rubbish from their vehicle windows, contributing to a growing problem that affected both urban and rural landscapes. Common items thrown away included fast food wrappers, plastic and glass bottles, cigarette butts and even larger debris such as old tires and furniture. This litter not only marred the natural beauty of the surroundings but also posed significant threats to wildlife, as animals can ingest or become entangled in the debris.

Despite his exhaustion, Lothar remained focused on his mission, delivering a seed-cleaning machine to a farmer in need. With each turn of the wheel, the promise of a rewarding conclusion propelled him forward along the Kennedy Highway in Far North Queensland, carpeted with millions of cane toads.

In 1969, the "Keep Australia Clean" campaign began. It was established in response to growing concerns about litter and environmental degradation in Australia. The initiative aimed to raise awareness about littering and promote responsible waste disposal practices among Australians. Over the years, the campaign has evolved, incorporating various programs and activities to engage communities and encourage positive behaviour toward the environment. As environmental concerns grew, both public awareness and penalties for littering increased.

After seven years of life on the road, Lothar had become a true master of long-distance driving across the vast continent of Australia. He witnessed the transformation from a filthy environment into clean and orderly surroundings.

When he first began his journey, he was a nervous novice, unsure of his abilities. However, with determination and countless miles behind the wheel, Lothar had transformed into a seasoned driver and a mechanic.

Each highway in Australia held a story for him. He could navigate the Hume Highway with ease gliding past rolling green hills that transformed into golden fields. The Pacific Highway felt like an old friend, with its stunning coastal views and winding turns that hugged the cliffs above the turquoise sea. He reminisced about the starlit nights spent parked under the expansive sky, the only sounds being the distant crash of waves and the soft rustle of leaves.

Lothar carried a worn map in the glove compartment, not because he needed it, but as a comforting reminder of his early days when he relied on it to find his way. Now, he could name every major route and backroad from Sydney to Perth, from Cairns to Adelaide, his mind filled with the rhythm of numbers and names – Highways 1, 3 and many others rolled off his tongue like song lyrics.

He marvelled at how the rugged outback transformed with every journey. The bare red earth of the Northern Territory brought a sense of adventure he had never known. He could still feel the thrill of driving through the ochre sandsunder the midday sun, and the cool shade of a lone gumtree was a welcomed break from the heat.

Australian Gum Tree

Kangaroos in Australia

Lothar led a bustling life, dedicated to the grind of earning a living amidst the hustle and bustle of his daily routine. Juggling multiple responsibilities, he worked tirelessly to provide for himself and ensure a stable future. Despite the demands of his job, he made it a point to maintain a deep connection with his family back in Germany.

The distance between them was bridged by the time-honoured practice of letter writing. Each month, Lothar would take the time to pen thoughtful letters, pouring his thoughts and experiences onto the pages. He detailed the events of his life, sharing stories of his work and the challenges he faced as well as the small joys that brightened his days. In return, his mother would send her own letters, filled with warmth, love and updates about family happenings in Germany.

In her letters, Else expressed her longing for her son Lothar and inquired about his plans to return to Germany. "When are you coming back home.?" Her words carried a sense of nostalgia and hope, reflecting the close bond they shared. She likely recalled fond memories of their time together, highlighting the importance of family ties.

Lothar's response was clear and resolute. He firmly conveyed his decision. "I will not go back to Germany. I have a family here in Australia-a wife and two sons." His message conveyed not only his commitment to his new life but also a sense of belonging to his current surroundings. This statement reflected the challenges of balancing familial obligations with the realities of his life abroad, emphasizing the significance of his relationships in Australia. This exchange illustrates the complexities of migration, family ties, and the emotional weight of belonging, revealing a poignant moment between mother and son separated by distance but connected through their feelings.

Upon learning that Lothar intended to stay in Australia permanently, Else felt a profound sense of urgency and a desire to be closer to her son. This revelation ignited a spark within her, prompting the idea of migrating herself. She envisioned a new beginning, a chance to explore the life that Lothar had built.

However, her husband was opposed to the idea. He harboured concerns about leaving their familiar life in Germany, fearing the challenges of starting anew in a foreign land. The prospect of migration unsettled him, and he voiced his discontent, suggesting they should remain where they were.

Despite his reservations, Else stood her ground. Her determination shone through when she firmly stated, "If you don't want to migrate to Australia, I will leave you behind." Her words reflected not only her commitment to her son but also a willingness to prioritise her family connection over her marital relationship. This assertion highlighted the emotional stakes involved in the decision, revealing the depth of her love for Lothar and her readiness to embrace change, even at the risk of significant upheaval in her personal life.

THE LAST HORIZON

Else's determination to migrate to Australia solidified as she realised that the prospect of reuniting with Lothar and forging a new life outweighed the challenges they might face. With a sense of purpose, she communicated her unwavering decision to her husband.

Initially resistant, Else's husband gradually began to understand the depth of her feelings and the value of family connections. The thought of separating from Else was daunting, and as he reflected on the potential for new beginnings, he recognised the importance of supporting her dream.

Conversations with their son Wolfgang further influenced his perspective, as they both realised the opportunity for a shared adventure and the chance to create new memories together as a family. Eventually, both he and Wolfgang agreed to make the leap embracing the unknown alongside Else.

They resolved to migrate to Australia, excited yet apprehensive about the changes ahead. This united decision symbolised not only a commitment to family but also a willingness to adapt and thrive in a new environment where they could be close to Lothar and his family. The family's journey highlighted the importance of compromise, love, and the strength that comes from standing together in the face of change.

After relocating to Australia, Bill, Else and Wolfgang began a new chapter in their lives. Embracing their new surroundings, they quickly adapted to the local culture, making connections and establishing a sense of community. With a shared vision for the future, Bill and Wolfgang decided to venture into the trucking industry. They pooled their resources and expertise, setting up a trucking business that was well-received, thanks to their hard work and determination as well as Lothar's input.

Bill's gratitude for migrating to Australia was palpable as he reflected on the profound changes it brought to his family's life. The decision to move, once filled with uncertainty and apprehension, had blossomed into a journey of opportunity and growth.

As the trucking business flourished, Bill felt a sense of pride in their accomplishments. Bill also appreciated the opportunities available to Wolfgang. The growing enterprise allowed his son to develop skills, gain independence and carve his path in the world. With a combination of innovation and dedication, Wolfgang and his wife Sue expanded the business, investing in new trucks and technology to improve efficiency.

Lothar's appreciation for his parents' decision to join him in Australia deeply enriched his life. Their migration brought a palpable sense of warmth and support, creating a familial atmosphere that he had longed for while living abroad. With his parents close by, Lothar felt an invigorated sense of belonging that reignited his motivation and drive. Their presence reminded him of the importance of family values, pushing him to aim higher and strive for greater achievements in his personal and professional life.

Consequently, Lothar's ambition rose significantly, fuelled by the love and support from the family he cherished.

After several years of building a life in Australia, Else faced a challenging battle with cancer. Despite the warmth of the sun and the support of her family, her health began to decline, leading to a hospitalisation that marked a difficult chapter in their lives. In her last moments, as the weight of her illness became too much to bear, Else found solace in the presence of her family.

When Lothar's mother finally succumbed to her illness, he held her tightly in his arms. In that heart-wrenching moment, they shared a silent promise that her spirit would live on in his heart, guiding him as he navigated life without her.

Jackknifing

Truck Driving Mishaps on the Open Road

Lothar's driving career was in its fifth year when one afternoon, while cruising along the Stuart Highway, he took a moment to reflect as he passed through bare stretches of land speckled with wildflowers. He had not just learned the routes, but also the heart of the land. He met fellow truck drivers who had become his lifelong friends and confidants. Each connection deepened his appreciation for the people and places of Australia.

As sunset approached, painting the sky with vibrant hues of orange and purple, Lothar parked his truck along the rugged roadside to stretch his legs and have a little break. He stepped out, inhaling deeply the fresh, earthy scent of the landscape. As he approached his vehicle, he noticed a Border Collie perched comfortably in the passenger seat, its expressive eyes watching him curiously.

This unexpected encounter transformed into a delightful companionship, as the loyal dog quickly became Lothar's driving partner for the next few months. The dog's unwavering loyalty provided a sense of comfort and joy during Lothar's travels.

As Lothar drove past the familiar stretch of road in Southern Queensland where he had first discovered the Border Collie, a sense of nostalgia washed over him. But this time, the dog was filled with undeniable excitement.

In a flash, the Collie leaped from the passenger seat, bounding toward an expansive open field, its fur catching the sunlight as it raced ahead. Lothar called after the dog, his voice echoing against the backdrop of the landscape, but the Border Collie was captivated by the thrill of freedom. With each stride, it sprinted farther away, tail high with joy, ignoring Lothar's calls.

Panic began to rise in Lothar's chest as he watched the dog's silhouette grow smaller against the vastness of the field. He could see the dog weaving through the tall grass, its instincts kicking n as it explored the world around it. Despite his attempts to coax it back, Lothar was left standing by the roadside, torn between the happiness of the dog's unrestrained spirit and the concern for its safety.

Lothar drove on. He realised he had become more than just a driver, he had become part of the vast tapestry of Australia. The highways and roads were etched in his memory, a solid bridge between him and the breathtaking beauty they led to. There was a comforting certainty in the journey itself, and with a smile, he knew he would keep driving.

As Lothar continued his hauling business, the days turned into weeks, and a month passed since the spirited Border Collie had dashed away into the open field. Now, he found himself parked 200 kilometres from that memorable spot in Morgan, weary yet determined, and in need of a break. It was almost midnight when he stepped into the restroom, the stillness of the night enveloping him. Upon returning to his truck, fatigue momentarily faded into disbelief. There, nestled comfortably in the passenger seat, was the same Border Collie, tail wagging furiously and eyes sparkling with recognition.

Bisquit the Border Collie

Lothar's heart swelled with joy as he opened the door, and the dog leapt into his arms, a whirlwind of excitement and love. This unexpected reunion felt like a miracle, erasing the worries of the past month. Grinning from ear to ear, Lothar petted the dog's thick fur, grateful for the wonderful twist of fate. With a newfound sense of companionship, he set off on the road once again, making his way home to Adelaide, South Australia with his loyal friend by his side, ready for countless new adventures together.

As the miles unfurled beneath Lothar, he realised he had been driving for seven years across the continent. He sat at his kitchen table, a notebook sprawled open in front of him, filled with notes and calculations. The afternoon sunlight streamed through the window, casting a warm glow on the worn pages that chronicled his recent journeys.

He had felt increasingly burdened by the demands of his driving job, and today, he decided to take a closer look at the numbers. As he began to tally his hours behind the wheels, his brow furrowed in concentration. Each journey was meticulously recorded – some long stretches on highways, other nimble navigations through city streets. He scribbled down the total hours spent driving, calculating the miles covered, the fuel costs, and the wear and tear of his vehicle.

With each number he wrote, Lothar felt a growing sense of unease. The miles travelled were considerable and the hours spent on the road blurred together into a relentless cycle of driving, loading and unloading. He reflected on the challenges he often faced: unexpected detours due to construction, the frustrations of heavy traffic during rush hour, the occasional runin with difficult clients who demanded more than what was promised.

After compiling all the data, Lothar took a deep breath and weighed his total earnings against the extensive hours put in and the numerous challenges he faced. The stark realisation hit him hard: the numbers didn't add up in his favour. The hours he'd poured into driving, the distances he'd traversed, and the challenges he'd navigated were all incredibly taxing, yet his earnings were disappointingly low. A wave of frustration washed over him.

Lothar had always prided himself on hard work, believing that dedication would eventually yield success. Yet, here he was, faced with the harsh truth that sometimes effort and reward did not align. This realisation forced him to reconsider his approach.

THE LAST HORIZON

He thought about his family, his future – the long nights spent on the road, the toll it took on his personal life, and whether the sacrifices were worth the pay. Lothar leaned back in his chair, staring at the calculations laid out before him. Determined, he resolved to find a solution, whether it meant seeking better opportunities or adjusting his current approach to driving.

Today marked not just a day of calculations, but also the beginning of a new journey towards a more fulfilling chapter in his professional life. He developed a thirst for new challenges that surpassed the monotony of the open road.

One day, he passed a charming liquor shop nestled by the roadside, its vibrant sign flickering in the sun. The idea struck him like a bolt of lightning. What if he could turn his passion for adventure into a thriving business? After some soul-searching, Lothar sold his truck and bought the liquor shop, pouring his energy into its transformation.

He curated an eclectic selection of local wines and international spirits, creating a welcoming haven for travellers and locals alike. Word spread quickly and the little shop became a gathering spot, filled with laughter and warmth. Lothar thrived in his new venture, finding joy not just in running a business but in the connections he forged. Lothar revelled in the vibrant life of his liquor shop, the laughter of customers and the clinking of bottles creating a melody that filled the air. Each day brought new faces and stories, and he savoured every moment.

One warm afternoon, a sharply dressed stranger entered, his gaze scanning the shelves with an intense interest. "I'd like to buy your business," the stranger stated plainly, his confidence palpable. Lothar chuckled, shaking his head. "This business is not for sale." But the stranger leaned closer. "I will be back tomorrow to offer you an amount that you could not refuse. See you then."

Lothar's Love of Liquor

The following day, the stranger came back. Curiosity piqued. Lothar listened as the stranger unveiled a sum that sent his heart racing. It was beyond anything he had envisioned. The thrill of the challenge he had embraced now wavered against the allure of newfound possibilities. After a moment of contemplation, Lothar nodded, the decision settling in his chest like a stone. "Alright." he said reluctantly shaking the stranger's hand to seal the deal. As he handed over the keys, he felt a pang of nostalgia. But with every ending comes a new beginning.

CHAPTER 8
BACK TO THE SPOTLIGHT

A new beginning awaited him in Adelaide, South Australia where he returned to work in the Adelaide Festival Theatre as a stage technician; a job that felt as familiar as an old friend. The scent of fresh paint and polished wood greeted him transporting him back to 1959 when he had left Germany, filled with dreams and uncertainties. Despite the decades that had passed, nothing seemed to have changed fundamentally. Lothar resumed his role as a stage technician, a job he had loved long ago. As he moved through the theatre with ease, setting up various performances, he marvelled at the circularity of it all.

On breaks, he would sit on the plush red seats, watching the world-renowned performers like Russian ballet dancers Mikhail Baryshnikov and Rudolf Nureyev hone their craft. As he poured his heart into the job surrounded by creativity and dreams, he found a profound sense of peace.

Lothar glanced around the Adelaide Festival Theatre, savouring the familiar sights and sounds that had accompanied him for the past five years. The bustling world of stage technicians, where shadows danced and lights flickered to life, felt like home. But recently, a nagging sense of restlessness had settled in his chest. It was time for a change.

Foundations of Care: Lothar's Journey in Building Nursing Homes

Having established himself in the real estate development business over the years, he was determined to expand his horizons even further. With a vision that extended beyond simple profit, Lothar embarked on a mission to build not only properties but also communities.

Being inspired by his friend Ron Tonkin, his first major project was a nursing home designed to meld comfort and care. He worked closely with experts to ensure the facility had not just the necessary health infrastructures but also a environment that felt like home. The home's design included lush gardens and open spaces that invited nature inside, fostering peace and connection.

The Homestead Nursing Home was established in 1980. The original plan was for sixty beds built in two stages. The first stage consisting of thirty beds was completed in October 1980 and the second stage also consisting of thirty beds was completed in 1982 making the overall bed capacity of sixty, as originally intended.

THE LAST HORIZON

Lothar first conceived of the Homestead style as he felt it would blend in with the country atmosphere. The building was purposely built with wide corridors surrounding central courtyards providing outside access from most areas of the nursing home. The courtyards were developed with an abundance of plants and shrubs for the benefit of residents who wished to sit quietly in a garden setting. Mr. Konzag, one of the residents, attended to the gardening.

Lothar's vision for the nursing home came to fruition as the construction was completed, creating a warm and welcoming space for residents to call home. Eager to enhance the environment, he recognised the importance of art in fostering a comforting and uplifting atmosphere. Lothar's desire to hang paintings on the walls was fuelled by the belief that vibrant artwork could inspire joy and spark nostalgia among the residents. However, as he prepared to adorn the nursing home with beautiful creations, Lothar faced a financial hurdle, as he did not have the funds necessary to purchase paintings.

Undeterred by this setback, he decided to channel his creativity and resourcefulness. He purchased essential material – canvas, paints, brushes and other supplies – determined to create a collection of artworks that would brighten the residence. With a sense of purpose, Lothar rolled up his sleeves and began painting.

He poured his heart into each piece drawing inspiration from nature, memories, and the vibrant tapestry of life. Over time, he skilfully crafted fifty-six unique paintings, each reflecting different themes and emotions. Some paintings depicted serene landscapes, while others showcased abstract patterns filled with bold colours. They all shared a common goal; to evoke a sense of warmth and connection among the residents. Once completed, Lothar eagerly hang the paintings on the walls of the nursing home, transforming the sterile environment into a gallery of creativity and expression.

The Homestead Nursing Home had a staff of seventy-two comprising sisters, nurses, domestics, cooks, laundry staff, a handyman and gardener. The Director of Nursing was Mr Gary McKiernan, Deputy of Nursing Sr Anne O'Cornell, Receptionist Chris Clarke, and Housekeeper and Activities Supervisor, Dianne McKiernan.

Within the nursing home a fundraising committee was developed, known as the Homestead Activity Group (HAG) which was made up of twelve volunteer staff members. This group organised activities to raise funds to subsidise extras for the residents, such as buying an organ, Easter eggs, Christmas presents, film and the developing of photos taken of residents at various times during the year, and buying perms for the hairdressing salon.

A competition was advertised in the local paper which resulted in the designing of the banner. The words and colours for the banner were chosen by the residents themselves adding to the original design by Doug Tucker.

Events composed of a fashion parade in August, residents Picnic Day in Adelaide in October, Melbourne Cup afternoon tea in November and the residents' Christmas Party in December.

The fashion parade was held over three days and advertised in the local paper, all stocks arriving from Sydney was available to purchase on the night.

The Melbourne Cup afternoon tea was open to the public and prizes were awarded for the best novelty hats and also featured in the local newspaper.

The Christmas party was given each year and residents invited friends and relatives to the Christmas dinner where Father Christmas arrived giving gifts to all residents.

The nursing home was a continuation of home life as much as possible and every care was taken to provide as much support and security as needed. Individuals and groups in the community were encouraged to frequent the nursing home and become involved with the residents which in turn "brings them out" into the community with words and social contact.

Within the Nursing Home a programme was organised to try to cater for the needs of all residents:

Monday Morning – Table tennis; afternoon – craft Tuesday Morning – Exercises; afternoon – team games Wednesday Morning- bingo ; afternoon – yoga Thursday Morning – Exercises; afternoon -ceramics Friday Morning – indoor bowls; afternoon-craft

Flush with the success of the first nursing home, he built another. Before long, Lothar's nursing home became the largest employer in Kadina. By prioritising local talent, he empowered families and enriched the community.

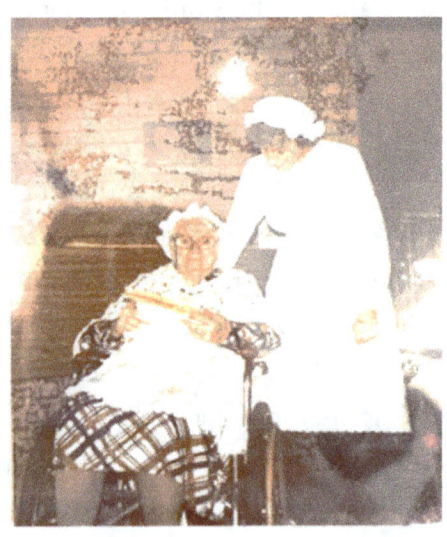

Homestead Nursing Home Resident

Building Dreams, Losing Love

Amid rebuilding properties and crafting a life defined by hard work and dedication, Lothar found his marriage slowly unravelling. As he devoted his days to fixing buildings, investing not only in materials but also in his aspirations, the emotional foundation of his relationship with Helga began to show signs of stress. Despite their shared dreams and the twenty-one years spent together, it became increasingly clear that they were growing apart.

Recognising the shift in their relationship, Lothar and Helga chose to approach the situation with maturity and respect. Instead of allowing misunderstandings and resentment to escalate, they engaged in open conversations about their feelings and the future of their marriage.

In a world where divorce can often be acrimonious, Lothar and Helga opted for an amicable separation. They made a decision that reflected their mutual respect and desire for a peaceful resolution. Rather than engaging in a contentious legal battle, they chose to approach the separation with a spirit of collaboration and understanding.

In a quiet moment together, Lothar looked at Helga and said, "I want you to have the freedom to choose which of our properties you'd like to keep." This gesture was not just about assets; it was an acknowledgment of their shared memories and the life they had shared together for twenty-one years. They had worked hard throughout their marriage, and Lothar wanted to ensure Helga felt valued, even as their paths diverged.

Helga appreciated Lothar's thoughtful approach. Together, they reviewed their properties -each one holding its own story and significance. They discussed the pros and cons of each location, weighing emotional attachments against practical considerations. In that moment, the tension that often accompanies divorce felt noticeably lighter.

They agreed the distribution would be equal, reflecting their commitment to fairness and equity. This decision brought a sense of relief to both. They had always believed in partnership, and even in parting, they chose to honour that.

Ultimately, Helga decided on a property that felt like home to her, a place where she could continue to build her future. Lothar took the other properties, each a testament to their shared efforts.

As they finalised their decisions, an unusual calm settled between them. There were no lawyers involved, no long battles over possessions, and no lingering animosities. Instead, their conversations were marked by understanding and a mutual sense of closure.

With their responsibilities settled, Lothar and Helga parted ways with a sense of peace. They knew that they were embarking on separate journeys but could look back on their shared years with appreciation, having chosen respect and harmony over conflict.

CHAPTER 9
A JOURNEY OF REINVENTION

Lothar stood before the worn-out blocks of industrial property nestled on a 10,000 square metre block of land in Hindmarsh. Its faded bricks and cracked windows were telling stories of a once-thriving past. As he gazed at the decay, a spark of ambition ignited within him. This structure, long forgotten and nearly crumbling would become his canvas. Drawing on the bricklaying and carpentry skills he had learned in Germany as a young man, he rolled up his sleeves and got to work.

Each morning, sunlight spilled through the dust-laden air, illuminating the rough textures of the aged bricks. He felt a connection to the past, each brick he laid carried the weight of history, while every beam he crafted spoke of new possibilities. With careful hands, Lothar repaired the walls, replacing the damaged bricks and mending the wooden frames.

One Saturday morning, Lothar found himself alone on the roof of a unit he had been refurbishing. The sun shone brightly, casting warm rays across the steel frame he perched on, six metres above the ground. He diligently worked, securing the last few panels when suddenly, there was a creak. The twenty-foot steel beam gave way. Time seemed to slow as he plunged downward.

Lothar landed with a sickening thud. Pain exploded in his foot, as the heavy steel beam crashed onto him. Stars danced before his eyes and the world faded. As it was happening, his friend Max Wessel happened to pass by. He immediately sensed something was terribly wrong when he saw Lothar sprawled on the ground with a bleeding and mangled foot, the frame lying beside him. Panic ignited within Max. He called an ambulance.

Lothar's accident was a stark reminder of life's unpredictability. As he fell from the roof, the impact left his right foot severely crushed, leading him to the hospital where the gravity of his situation began to unfold. The doctor, assessing Lothar's injury, delivered a surprising but hopeful message: "You are lucky."

He went on to explain that during his previous experience in the Vietnam war zone, he would have had no choice but to amputate the crushed foot, as medical resources and options had been severely limited in such dire environments. However, advancements in medicine now provided the opportunity to reconstruct Lothar's right foot, a testament on how far the medical field has progressed.

This situation posed a significant challenge, yet it also sparked a sense of optimism. The reconstruction would not only test the capabilities of modern surgery but would also serve as a beacon of hope for Lothar, symbolising resilience and the evolving nature of medical practices. Lothar's one year journey from injury to recovery would become a story of transformation, reflecting both personal strength and the promise of medical advancements.

Lothar's life was saved and his right foot reconstructed.

Lothar's curiosity was piqued as he learned about his friends Ron and Jo acquiring properties in Far North Queensland. Their animated stories of lush landscapes, crystal-clear waters and vibrant wildlife painted a picture of paradise that captivated his imagination. He listened intently as they shared their experiences, painting vivid images of the tropical beauty and unique lifestyle that characterised the region.

As Lothar delved deeper into their tales, he became increasingly enchanted by the allure of the tropics. The contrast between the bustling cities and the serene unspoiled nature of Cape Tribulation sparked a longing within him. Motivated by his new-found fascination, Lothar decided to pursue his dream of building a resort in Cape Tribulation.

With a clear vision and an eagerness to embrace this new chapter, Lothar set forth on his journey to create a haven in the breathtaking surroundings of Cape Tribulation, eagerly anticipating all the adventures and connections that awaited him along the way. Cape Tribulation is approximately 110 kilometres north of Cairns. It is situated within the Daintree National Park where The Great Barrier Reef meets the Rainforest, creating one of the world's most unique ecosystems.

Cape Tribulation is renowned for its stunning natural scenery, including pristine beaches, lush rainforest and coral reefs. It has a beautiful beach where visitors can enjoy swimming, snorkelling, and relaxing in a stunning natural setting. Part of the world's oldest tropical forest, the Daintree Rainforest, is home to diverse flora and fauna. There are several walking trails for those who want to explore the surrounding rainforest such as the Dubuji Boardwalk and the Mount Sorrow Ridge Trail. The area is rich in wildlife, including cassowaries, tree kangaroos and various bird species.

It is a popular destination for eco-tourism, attracting visitors interested in its natural beauty and biodiversity. It is also an important area for conservation efforts aimed at protecting its unique ecosystems. The road to Cape Tribulation was notably blocked for six weeks by conservationists in 1983. This action was part of a broader movement to protect the Daintree Rainforest, which is a UNESCO world heritage site known for its unique biodiversity. The blockade drew significant attention to the environmental issues surrounding the area and led to discussions about conservation and sustainable development.

In 1984, Lothar laid down plans for a getaway resort that would offer a perfect blend of relaxation and adventure. Nestled among palm trees and overlooking azure waters where the mountain meets the sea, the resort would cater to backpackers from all over the world seeking both tranquillity and activities including snorkelling, hiking, local wildlife tours and night life filled with dancing and music.

Lothar's PK Jungle Village Resort provided an adventurous blend of stunning natural beauty, rich cultural experiences, and a lively social scene, making it desirable destination for travellers seeking both excitement and relaxation. backpackers had a common conception that they should reach Cape Tribulation to be called a *'real backpacker'*. That is the reason why Lothar's resort was always full to capacity.

To reach the area, many travellers opt to rent a car for the flexibility it provides. Driving along the scenic coastal roads allows for stops at picturesque views and hidden beaches. A popular choice among backpackers are campervans enabling them to experience an adventurous road trip while providing accommodation. Budget-friendly buses take passengers from Cairns to Cape Tribulation.

For those seeking a bit of a thrill, renting a motorbike is an exhilarating option. Some backpackers bring or rent bicycles, enjoying a more intimate exploration of the region. Cycling through the lush rainforest can lead to unique encounters with wildlife. For the adventurous spirit, trekking from nearby spots can be a great way to reach Cape Tribulation. For reaching more isolated areas of the reef and nearby islands, some opt for boat tours that depart from locations like Port Douglas.

Once at the resort, backpackers can enjoy activities like hiking, swimming, snorkelling, and exploring the Daintree Rainforest. The laid-back atmosphere often fosters community among travellers, making it a memorable part of the journey.

Mark and Pierre, two vibrant sons of Lothar with a knack of bringing people together, took it upon themselves to organise social activities for the guests. Their enthusiasm was contagious, and they aimed to create an unforgettable atmosphere filled with laughter and camaraderie.

Every evening, as the sun dipped below the horizon, the central gathering area transformed into a lively limbo zone. They set up a brightly coloured limbo stick, and participants took turns bending backward to see how *low they could go* while groovy tunes played in the background. Cheerful cheers and playful banter filled the air, fostering the spirit of friendly competition.

With professional speakers and an eclectic mix of music, Mark and Pierre turned the open space into a disco paradise. From classic hits to contemporary dance tracks, backpackers danced under the stars. The infectious rhythms had everyone moving, and even those who were initially shy found themselves swept up in the joy of the moment.

To ramp up the energy, they organized a spirited beer-drinking contest, encouraging participants to compete in teams. Laughter erupted as participants engaged in playful challenges, from speed-drinking to unique games that involved balancing cups. The friendly rivalry brought strangers closer together, sparking conversations and forming new friendships.

One genuine friendship formed was between Mark and Peter from Holland who treated each other like real brothers and business partners when they left Cape Tribulation.

The air was filled with a mix of excitement and laughter as backpackers from various corners of the globe united in the festivities. Conversations flowed as easily as the music, with people sharing stories of their travels while making lasting memories. As night deepened, the activities created a vibrant tapestry of youthful exuberance, cementing Mark and Pierre's reputation as the ultimate hosts. The social events not only showcased the beauty of the surroundings but also celebrated the spirit of adventure that defined their backpacking journey. It was a perfect blend of fun and fellowship, marking Cape Tribulation as a highlight in their travels.

In the stillness of the night in Cape Tribulation, the serene sounds of the rainforest were suddenly interrupted by the arrival of two Swedish backpackers. Their laughter echoed as they emerged from the shadows, gleaming with excitement from their adventure.

Lothar welcomed them and couldn't help but inquire, "How did you cross the Daintree River? The ferry is closed now." With a mixture of pride and nonchalance, one of the ladies replied, "we swam."

Lothar's expression shifted from curiosity to concern. "So, you didn't know there are crocodiles in the river?" The two ladies exchanged bewildered glances, then responded in unison, "No!" Their eyes widened, realising the gravity of their decision.

The laughter faded, replaced by a moment of silence as they processed the risk they had taken. Surrounded by towering palm trees and the distant sound of wildlife, the stark contrast between their carefree spirit and the lurking dangers in the river created an intriguing dynamic. As they settled into the hostel for the night, the adrenaline of their nighttime swim mingled with the thrill of their newfound knowledge, turning a reckless adventure into a story they would share for years to come.

One of the saltwater crocodiles lurking in the Daintree River in Cape Tribulation Far North Queensland Australia.

Aerial View of Far North Queensland Australia

Lothar delved once again into the world of real estate. He poured his energy into understanding the market, reading a lot of books, talking to seasoned real estate agents and studying neighbourhoods. The thrill of analysing properties and envisioning their potential captivated him. He learned the three crucial 'Ps' in buying properties Position:*Position*; and Position.

Lothar purchased a picturesque property in Kuranda, nestled within the breathtaking Australian Rainforest. Renowned for its lush greenery and vibrant wildlife, this enchanting location was the perfect backdrop for his ambitious vision.

Kuranda is a village located in Far North Queensland, Australia, approximately 25 kilometres northwest of Cairns. Nestled in the rainforest of the Macalister Range, it is situated at an elevation of about 330 metres (1,080 feet) above sea level.

Kuranda is known for its stunning natural beauty, including lush rainforests, the Barron Falls and a vibrant local arts scene. Popular attractions include: Kuranda Scenic Railway – A picturesque train journey through the rainforest and vast waterfalls; Sky rail Rainforest Cableway – a gondola ride offering breathtaking views of the forest canopy; Kuranda Markets offering handmade crafts, local produce and souvenirs.

The village is a popular destination for both tourists and locals providing a unique experience of the tropical environment and indigenous culture.

Kuranda is home to a rich diversity of fauna including Cassowaries – the large flightless birds that are iconic to the region.

With towering trees swaying gently in the breeze and the distant sound of nature surrounding him, Lothar envisioned a thriving shopping centre that would not only serve as a hub for the locals but also attract tourists eager to experience the unique charm of Kuranda.

Lothar's ambitious project in the Kuranda Rainforest area required ingenuity and precision, particularly when it came to transporting materials to the elevated site. With the construction phase in full swing, he utilised a helicopter to effortlessly shuttle supplies across the rugged terrain.

The helicopter, a powerful machine with its rotor blades whirring fiercely, hovered above the shopping centre's framework, casting a broad shadow on the site below. With meticulous coordination, it manoeuvred into position, lowering the robust materials that would soon become the roofs of the shopping centre. Each load was carefully secured, the bright colours of tarps and slings contrasting vividly against the surrounding greenery. Below, a team of skilled riggers stood at the ready, clad in safety gear and equipped with harnesses and tools.

Their focus was unwavering as they communicated through hand signals and shouts, anticipating each movement of the helicopter. As the materials descended, the riggers sprang into action, working in perfect harmony to guide and fasten the heavy roofs with precision. The collective effort showcased their expertise, each person playing a crucial role in seamlessly orchestrating the installation.

Despite the challenges of working on such a steep and uneven landscape, the atmosphere buzzed with excitement and camaraderie. Lothar watched from a distance, a satisfied smile on his face as he witnessed the labour and teamwork that brought his vision closer to reality. "Nothing is impossible," he whispered to himself remembering the lessons from his former boss Albert Zotsman in the theatre in Germany The sight of the helicopter lifting off with another load was a reminder of the ambitious heights he aimed to reach, literally and figuratively, in transforming Kuranda into a thriving hub which he named *Kuranda Village Centre.*

Lothar's Kuranda Village Centre

THE LAST HORIZON

This Cassowary Replica is displayed in the Kuranda Information Centre across from Kuranda Village Bazaar of Lothar. Drivers must stop to let cassowaries cross the road safely.

CHAPTER 10
CURIOSITY UNBOUND: A JOURNEY INTO THE UNKNOWN

One glorious springtime day, Lothar discovered several letters in his mailbox addressed to the previous occupant of his apartment. Curiosity piqued, he decided to open one of the envelopes. Inside, he found a heartfelt letter from a teenager in the Philippines, expressing profound gratitude for the financial assistance she had received for her schooling.

As he read her words, Lothar felt a wave of empathy wash over him. Her aspirations and struggles resonated deeply, inspiring him to lend a hand. Without hesitation, he slipped $300 into an envelope and mailed it, hoping it would make a tangible difference in her education.

A few weeks later, he received a reply that warmed his heart. The student expressed her heartfelt thanks, sharing how the money had significantly alleviated her financial burden, enabling her to pay her tuition fees and other needs. Her joy and relief were palpable through her words, solidifying a bond that transcended distance and culture.

Inspired by the heartfelt letters, Lothar made the decision to meet the student he had been corresponding with in the Philippines. With excitement and anticipation, he booked his flight and set off on his journey to the stunning archipelago.

Upon arrival in Manila, he flew to Coron, a picturesque island in Palawan renowned for its crystal-clear waters, majestic limestone cliffs, and vibrant coral reefs. As he navigated through the fishing village and greeted the friendly locals, he felt a sense of adventure and connection that he longed for.

Cullion Island, Palawan, Philippines

The student's address was Cullion – the next island featuring secluded beaches with powdery white sand. When Lothar arrived in Cullion on a little outrigger boat, he learned that the island was once home to a leprosy colony established during the Spanish colonial era in the Philippines. He also learned that the student he wanted to meet had already flown back to her school in Manila.

Lothar met the girl in Manila and learned more about her life and culture. He realised that his small act of kindness not only supported the student's dreams but also enriched his own life, reminding him of the profound impact that simple gestures can have in connecting people across the globe.

Boracay Island Odyssey

After a couple of years, Lothar felt a strong pull to return to the Philippines, his heart still warmed by the connections he'd made. During his research, he discovered the enchanting Boracay Island, known for its stunning powdery white beaches and vibrant atmosphere.

Boracay Island is in Malay, Aklan, located in the central Philippines, specifically in the Western Visayas region. It is one of the 7,601 islands in the Philippines situated 315 kilometres or 196 miles south of Manila.

Boracay is a popular tourist destination, attracting visitors from around the world. The island is approximately 10.32 square kilometres or about 4 square miles. This small yet popular island is known for its stunning white beaches, and sunsets offering a unique palette that can evoke various emotions and moods.

Boracay is also known for its vibrant nightlife, water sports activities – 'paraw' sailing, kiteboarding, surfing, diving and various aqua sports making it a favoured destination for tourists around the world.

Boracay local sailing boat 'paraw' (by Ella and Ariel Gad)

Lothar chartered a small plane to fly to Boracay Island located in Malay, Aklan. He spent six hours inspecting the 10,000 square metres of land located right on the beach with a 'nipa' house in the middle of the property. Lothar was mesmerised by the gentle breeze from the hundreds of swaying coconut palms and the long Bulabog east side white beach and turquoise blue water teeming with marine life. Inspired by the island's beauty, Lothar made a bold decision – he would build a resort on the island.

Being convinced that the captivating beauty of the tropical paradise island has the potential to attract enormous number of tourists, Lothar agreed to enter into a joint venture with Mrs Gelito (the landowner) and her heirs.

Lothar inquired about his eligibility to invest in real estate, company laws, taxation, development rules, tourist department promotions and approvals, security and other relevant information.

To a non-Filipino citizen like Lothar, it was very difficult to find competent lawyers in Manila but luckily, he had the contact number of Odi, a proficient corporate lawyer from a reputable law firm. She understood the complexity of real estate development in the area. To get more detailed information about the property she personally talked to the local council in Boracay, and the Municipal and Provincial Assessor's Offices. She became aware that the island had no Land Titles only Tax Declaration Numbers. Odi provided comprehensive legal guidance throughout the process.

By law a foreigner could legally own 49% of a company that holds real estate. Lothar's lawyer strategised by taking 4% of the shares in trust giving Lothar the privilege to own a total of 53% control while the Gelito family had 47% ownership.

Through meticulous planning and expert advice, the lawyer played a pivotal role in transforming Lothar's vision into a viable project, guiding him toward successfully establishing his resort while ensuring adherence to all legal and ethical standards.

When real estate changes hands in the Philippines, all members of the selling family who potentially have a right of inheritance must sign the contract and give their approval which they did.

Upon the resolution of all issues, Lothar made an application for an Investor's Visa to give him legal right to enter and leave the country. Director Ramona Ty, of the Department of Tourism, personally processed his application and expedited its approval through the Department of Immigration, as a gesture of support to foreign investors like him.

With the help of the lawyer, a young flamboyant architect was appointed. After acquiring municipal and 'barangay' (local council) approvals for all engineering plans and calculations, the project started. With the advice of the architect, Lothar decided to build a resort in a typical Philippine style with 'nipa' (grass) roof and external brick walls covered with bamboo.

The first hurdle came when Lothar scheduled to clear the land and start the building process. Mrs Gelito's son-in-law did not want to relocate his house built in the middle of the property. He stubbornly refused to vacate the land for whatever reason.

To resolve the issue Lothar called a meeting and informed all the Gelito family members that it was early enough to cancel the whole project due to this kind of uncooperative behaviour. Lothar gave them twenty-four hours to make up their mind. Lothar told them that if he received a negative response, he would pull out of the deal and take all approvals and plans with him. He would advise the Department of Lands and Tourism of the situation. He left that afternoon for Manila where they could contact him after deciding.

The next day, Mrs. Gelito, the matriarch of the family informed Lothar that she arranged relocation of the house to a nearby piece of land. Mrs Gelito's son-in-law was furious but had no choice but to obey the old woman's instruction. They built a frame under the house and organized a crew of some seventy men standing next to each other to lift and carry the house 200 metres away from the construction site. This Filipino tradition of helping each other is called 'bayanihan'.

Lothar gave the construction job to Bebot de Pedro of Nabas who was a very experienced large construction builder. He worked hand in hand with electrical and plumbing specialist Engineer Pre. The workforce comprised of 150 construction workers and tradespersons. While the construction was in full swing, they had no time to go home so they built their own little humpies and brought their wives along to cook their food and wash their clothes.

They built the first eighteen fully self-contained units, the restaurant building and bar, dance floor and performing stage, swimming pool, laundry and generator house, deep well, septic tank and big sewerage plant. The water tank was built high enough to produce enough pressure for gravity feeding to all pipes and showers.

Clothes hanging along the fences and lines, smoke from the open fire stoves, children playing amongst the free running chicken pecking dirt to pick small bugs or worms using their beaks, transformed the construction site into a little gypsy camp. Construction workers carrying their lamps made from tightly bundled coconut leaves to catch fish in the shallow waters in the evening displayed the ingenuity of the locals.

There were no telephone or other communication facilities on the island but there was a 'one way' radio in Caticlan. To talk to someone in Manila Lothar had to go to the mainland, queue up and wait for his turn to use the 'one way' radio for a maximum limited time of five minutes.

To solve this communication issue, Lothar set up a 'one way' radio tower in the resort and another tower in a tall building in Manila.

There was no electricity on the island either. So, whilst the construction was underway Lothar went to Manila and bought a ton heavy generator set and had it delivered to mainland Caticlan beach – the gateway to Boracay.

The generator was packed in soundproof housing. Technically, a one-ton heavy generator set could not be hauled by small outrigger boats which were the only available mode of transportation from the mainland to the island of Boracay. However, the advice of Lothar's former theatre director in Germany saying "nothing is impossible" reverberated in Lothar's mind.

On the island, Lothar built the foundation and concrete floor of the generator house. Then on the mainland, he built a five-layer high bamboo raft measuring 10x10 metres wide in front of the generator on the beach in mainland Caticlan.

Upon completion, some thirty to forty men pulled and pushed the generator over planks and roller pipes onto the raft. The raft was then towed by an outrigger boat.

It was a gloriously fine day perfect for cruising across the calm Boracay strait. The tranquillity of the turquoise blue sea was a bit disturbed by the revving engine of the outrigger boat towing the generator on the bamboo raft into the tropical paradise, which was just thirteen kilometres away.

Lothar was feeling marvellous while the bamboo raft was floating on and steadily heading towards the island when all of a sudden halfway between Caticlan and Boracay the boat engine stopped. The skipper restarted the engine many times but to no avail. The strong current rapidly lugged the boat and raft towards the West Philippine Sea.

While the generator was floating farther away, an oncoming passing boat witnessed what was happening. The boat captain stopped to give one of Lothar's crew a free ride to the mainland. He then organised another boat to tow the generator to the resort construction site in Boracay.

The construction looked like a very huge operation. Every day, dozens of boats delivered gravel, cement, wood, bamboo and all construction materials.

Power tools were unavailable in the Philippines in the early 80's. All work was done manually. Concrete was mixed by hand and most of the concrete blocks were made on site, supervised by two persons who were responsible to count the shovels of cement to meet the engineer's specification. Timber was sawn and planed by hand. Drilling was done using a hand drill.

When Lothar went to Australia, he had purchased a high-quality electric saw, excited about its potential to enhance his carpentry projects. Lothar called in a skilled carpenter to use it. However, the carpenter was initially hesitant to use the new electric saw. His reluctance stemmed from a couple of concerns. First, he felt a bit nervous about operating the saw, as he was accustomed to traditional hand tools and had zero experience with electric equipment. The thought of using an unfamiliar machine created a sense of unease, as he worried about safety and the possibility of making a mistake.

Second, the carpenter was mindful of the implications that such efficiency could bring. Utilising the electric saw would enable him to complete his tasks much more quickly, potentially leading to a faster finish.

While this speed was advantageous, it also raised anxiety about running out of work and earnings. He decided not to use any electric tools.

In Australia, Lothar's stepdad Bill opened his German Restaurant located in Hawthorndene, South Australia while Lothar was constructing the Laguna de Boracay resort. Bill called it Wiesental. Being a connoisseur' of German cuisine, he could cook high quality traditional German food.

While enjoying his restaurant venture, Bill entrusted the transport business to Lothar's brother Wolfgang who was aiming to build a forwarding business. After a lot of hard work, he achieved his goal of setting up the Doser Freight Forwarding Company, a very successful business.

At the Boracay construction site, the builder asked Lothar the exact location of the pool. Without saying a word, Lothar took a piece of bamboo stick, walked in front of the restaurant building and drew a line in the sand avoiding palm trees as much as possible, with the exception of one tree. He drew a line around the tree that would become an island in the middle of the pool. With the eighteen metres long by ten metres wide pool, the builder was able to dig out a substantial amount of sand needed to elevate the floor of the restaurant building to 1.3 metres off the ground.

Sixty men worked together to mix and pour the concrete in one go and many people collected pebbles in riverbeds in the nearby towns to be used in lining the walls and floor. Filters, chlorination and pumps were bought from Iloilo City. The collaboration between Filipino ingenuity and Lothar's artistic talent led to the creation of a uniquely designed swimming pool that stands out as both functional and aesthetically pleasing.

Filipino ingenuity often shines through in the resourceful use of local materials and innovative design ideas that reflect the vibrant culture and natural surroundings.

To Lothar, manual labours like these were just a replication of his bricklaying apprenticeship in Germany after the Second World War. In the 1980's, Filipinos solely relied on manual labour due to the unavailability of modern construction techniques and training. This focus on hands-on skills reflects the traditional methods of construction prevalent in the country, where physical work is emphasized. While these labourers possess a strong work ethic and resilience, their experience often highlights challenges related to skill development, job safety and technological adaptation in an evolving industry.

After three long years of labour, sweat, and shared aspirations, construction was finally completed. The once-quiet area of Boracay now housed Lothar's Laguna de Boracay Village Resort, a testament to the hard work and sacrifices made by Lothar, the builders and their families.

As the grand opening approached, Lothar marvelled at the journey that had unfolded. The resort stood not only as a symbol of his dream but also as a monument to the community forged through collaboration and resilience. Each corner resonated with stories of the workers who had transformed it into reality, linking their lives to Lothar's vision in ways that would forever shape the future of Boracay. The first stage of development was finally finished and officially opened to the public. At the opening party, friends, families, construction workers, government officials, marketing teams and tourist operators attended.

Lothar juggled his time travelling to look after his nursing home business in South Australia, PK Jungle Resort in Far North Queensland, Kuranda Village Shopping Centre in Kuranda, Far North Queensland Australia and Laguna de Boracay Resort in the Philippines.

THE LAST HORIZON

The 4.5 km long white beach in Boracay Island, Malay, Aklan, Philippines

Lothar's sixteen years in Boracay Island were not without their struggles. As he faced personal challenges, the weight of uncertainty bore down on him. Feeling overwhelmed, he contemplated giving up on the dream he had worked so hard to build. Each day was a battle, and as he prayed for divine intervention, he remained steadfast, unwilling to let his hard-earned investment go to waste. Lothar faced disappointment as his expectations of a surge in tourist arrivals dwindled, with most visitors being budget-conscious backpackers. Local tourists also struggled to afford his resort's rates, leading to financial struggles. Amidst these challenges and a failed romantic relationship, Lothar contemplated abandoning his investment. However, he resolved to stay a bit longer on the island holding onto hope for a better future.

One bright sunny day, a Dutch guy named Ronald Van Doggener turned up with the aim of convincing Lothar to sell the resort rooms through 'timeshare'. Mentally and physically exhausted he ignored him, but Ronald stayed in the resort for a whole month. Being a salesman, he knew that by pure probability and numbers, Lothar would listen to him at one stage. And so, it happened.

One very relaxing day, he listened to Ronald's explanation on how

'Timeshare Business" works. He told him that he and his Belgian partner had been selling Timeshares in the Canary Islands for several years and they needed resort units in the Philippines to expand their business.

Ronald successfully persuaded Lothar to transform Laguna de Boracay into a timeshare business model. By highlighting the potential for increased revenue and attracting a broader range of tourists, Ronald helped Lothar see the benefits of offering partial ownership, which would provide guests with more flexible vacation options and a more sustainable income stream for the resort. This strategic shift aimed to revitalise Lothar's struggling business and attract a steady clientele encouraging Lothar to lodge an application with the World Time Share Organisation Asia based in Singapore. The Time Share Organisation team visited the resort, suggested some changes and approved Lothar's application.

In the first year Lothar tried to sell timeshare in Germany and Austria but only a few 'weeks'were sold. Then Lothar teamed up with the British, Yugoslav and Dutch sales team who had just come back from a five year stint in Russia selling timeshares successfully.

"Where would you sell our time shares"? Lothar asked. "Right here in Manila" was their reply. Lothar said: "That's impossible". "There is plenty of money in Manila and you just have to find it" Within the span of eight months, there were 400 agents on the sales team competently marketing and selling 'timeshare weeks'. Within two years, over 1000 timeshare weeks were sold.

Despite finally starting to earn money from his resort, Lothar felt emotionally unfulfilled and unhappy. Recognising that financial success did not equate to personal happiness, he made the difficult decision to leave and seek a new direction for his life.

Just when he thought about losing hope, an unexpected opportunity arose. Ronald, from the timeshare company, approached Lothar with an interest in buying his resort. This offer felt like a beacon of light breaking through the clouds of despair. Lothar realised that his prayers to the 'Árchitect of the

Universe' were being answered, and with a sense of relief and gratitude, he agreed to the sale.

As he prepared to leave Boracay and return to Australia for good, Lothar experienced a whirlwind of emotions. It was a bittersweet goodbye to a place that had been both a dream and a challenge.

However, fate had one more surprise in store for him. During his final days on the island, Lothar met a woman named Maggie – the voice on the local radio. Maggie was enduring the painful realities of domestic violence while looking after her daughter Mycah and son, Monreo. Her strength and resilience in the face of adversity touched Lothar deeply. He found himself drawn to her, compelled to help in any way he could. The connection between them grew, and Lothar realised he had fallen in love.

Determined to provide her and her children with a safe and brighter future, Lothar sponsored their move to Australia. Their bond blossomed as they navigated life together in a new country, built on mutual support and understanding.

Eventually, their love culminated in a heartfelt wedding ceremony witnessed by two significant people, Wolfgang and Sue Doser, marking the beginning of a new chapter in both their lives. Lothar's journey, once filled with challenges and uncertainty, evolved into a story of love, resilience and second chances.

As they began their life together, Lothar understood that his time in Boracay had not been in vain. The trials he faced led him not just to a successful resolution, but to the love of his life who is willing to be with him until the last horizon appears. This is a testament to the unpredictable yet beautiful journey of life.

As he reflected on his journey, Lothar felt a profound sense of fulfillment. His dream had become a reality, showcasing the transformative power of dedication, cultural exchange, and the human spirit.

While managing his businesses successfully, Lothar's thirst for adventure did not wane. He caught wind of a private pilot's course as a New Year's resolution. The idea of soaring through the skies, looking down at the world from above, resonated deeply within him. With his characteristic determination, despite his age, Lothar enrolled, working arduous hours to balance his entrepreneurial responsibilities with his quest for knowledge.

After rigorous training and tireless study, the day finally arrived for his solo flight. With a heart pounding with adrenaline, Lothar prepared for his first solo flight. He conducted the pre-flight checks, his hands trembling slightly as he secured the hatch and climbed into the cockpit. The engine roared into life, a throaty growl that echoed his adventurous spirit. He took off, the ground falling away beneath him, revealing a tapestry of fields and forests sprawled below. But as he flew higher, the excitement morphed into unease.

Navigating through the air felt different without his instructor beside him. Every sound and every shift in the wind took on more significance. It didn't take long for the landmarks he'd memorised to transform into an indistinguishable blur. Clouds obscured his view and the compass seemed more of a suggestion than a guide. Panic gripped him as he circled helplessly, seeking solace in familiar sights that were nowhere to be seen. "Focus, Lothar. You can do this," he murmured to himself, recalling the lessons of his kind instructor. He took deep breaths, willing himself to think clearly.

It was time to return to the basics, find a reference point, rely on instruments, and above all, trust himself. After a few minutes that felt like hours, he spotted the railway line – a landmark he knew well.

With renewed purpose, he adjusted his course and followed the railway line, navigating his way back. The ground began to take shape and soon he was descending toward the airfield. As Lothar touched down, relief washed over him, intermingled with the raw thrill of a close call. The plane rolled to a stop, and he felt the tremors of anxiety begin to dissipate.

Yet, unlike the rush he imagined would follow, a heavy stillness enveloped his heart. The adrenaline faded, leaving a contemplative silence. Lothar unbuckled his harness and stepped out of the cockpit, staring at the plane in sombre reflection.

He had conquered this flight, but the fear of being lost alone in the vastness of the sky lingered in his thoughts. Despite the initial resolve to fly again, he found comfort on the ground. The thrill of altitude and the freedom of flight transformed into memories.

Lothar had always been captivated by the thrill of adventure, and his pursuit of new experiences had led him down some exciting paths. With a burgeoning real estate business at his fingertips, he often found himself longing for the exhilaration and freedom that came with mastering new skills. Therefore, he decided to dive into the world of skiing. His snow skiing began in Austria, the cradle of Alpine skiing.

With the majestic peaks of the Tyrol region surrounding him, Lothar took his first steep descent. The crisp air filled his lungs, and laughter echoed in the snowy valleys as he swished between fir trees, the sound of his skis carving the fresh snow. Next, he ventured to the Italian Dolomites.

The scenery was breathtaking, with towering cliffs sand charming chalets dotting the landscape. In Canada, Lothar encountered the rugged beauty of the Whistler. The sprawling ski resort boasted a diverse range of terrains, and Lothar relished every moment. He embraced the thrill of morning runs on freshly groomed slopes.

He also journeyed to the United States, where he tackled the breathtaking Rockies in Colorado. The stunning views and adrenaline recognised the changing seasons: the twinkling lights of Aspen were mesmerizing against the twilight sky.

In Australia, he enjoyed skiing in Falls Creek with his family and friends. Each winter became a chapter in a tale of adventure, friendship and passion for the mountains until he had a very bad fall in the Dolomites that made him decide to give up snow skiing.

Aside from skiing, Lothar had always been enchanted by the ocean's mysteries. After completing his scuba diving certification, he joined his colleagues for a weekend adventure beneath the waves. Their laughter echoed through the waters as they explored vibrant coral reefs and played with curious sea creatures. With each dive, Lothar's confidence grew, and he soon became a member of the British Sub-Aqua Club.

His adventures took him to breathtaking destinations – Boracay's crystal clear waters, Bali's stunning marine life, Greece's ancient underwater ruins, Tahiti's magical marine environment, and the diverse ecosystems surrounding Kangaroo Island and Victor Harbour in South Australia. Every dive was a new chapter in his life, filled with colourful fish, playful dolphins and the serenity of weightlessness.

Lothar's first dive in Papeete, Tahiti was nothing but magical. As he descended into the crystal-clear waters of the Pacific, he was greeted by a brilliant display of marine life. Tropical fish swirled around him like confetti, while vibrant corals painted the ocean floor. He spotted a majestic manta ray gliding gracefully above him, its wings flowing through the water like silk. He also found himself in Corfu, Greece where the warm Mediterranean sun cast a golden hue on the sea.

As Lothar submerged beneath the waves, he was captivated by the underwater caves and ancient ruins that lay beneath the surface. While Papeete showcased the vibrancy of tropical life, Corfu offered whispers of history and serenity. He was enamoured by the underwater world.

But he heard news of multiple shark attacks along the coast. His heart sank further when his friend recounted a harrowing tale of a narrow escape from a shark's terrifying bite. The vivid imagery of danger danced in Lothar's mind, eclipsing the beauty of the ocean he once cherished. Anxiety enveloped him like a thick fog; the thrill of diving turned to dread.

Lothar's Playground

CHAPTER 11
RENEWED LIFE

On Lothar's annual medical check-up, his GP discovered his Prostate Specific Antigen (PSA) level was 7.3 and it had increased more than 1% during the last year. She referred Lothar immediately to the urologist. The urologist decided to do biopsies on his prostate to determine the cause of the PSA's speedy increase.

The urologist took twelve biopsies from all parts of his prostate to be able to detect tumour malignancy – a very uncomfortable procedure. The result showed three suspicious areas. This meant that three biopsies needed to be taken after six weeks to give the prostate some rest from the previous shock.

Anxiety slowly crept into Lothar's whole being. The three biopsies taken revealed the presence of three tumours, all of which were confined to the prostate. This diagnosis highlighted the need for further evaluation and potential treatment options for his condition.

The urologist suggested the most common treatment - Radical Prostatectomy. In this procedure, the entire prostate is removed to make sure no regrowth can take place. Otherwise, his prognosis was only to live for another five years.

The words echoed in his mind, heavy and suffocating. "Five years." That was the prognosis – the time he had left to embrace life as he always knew it. At first, despair clouded Lothar's thoughts. He felt like a ship adrift in a stormy sea, lost and afraid.

To adhere to the professional ethics in dealing with patients, the urologist suggested he get a second opinion. Lothar quickly flew to the Epworth Hospital in Melbourne to see one of the top specialists. He suggested Robotic Surgery to minimise blood loss during the operation. Prostate tumours grow very slowly so Lothar also had the option to choose the 'wait and watch' attitude. However, he was fully aware that it was crucial for him to decide and choose his preferred treatment method.

Believing that knowledge is power Lothar bought all kinds of books about prostate cancer and its treatment. As he read the books, he became aware of prostate cancer treatments like prostate removal by surgical operation, radical prostatectomy, robotic surgery, radiation external beam therapy, radioactive seed implants, hormone treatment and chemotherapy.

Delving deeply into each kind of treatment Lothar discovered that all treatments had side-effects - incontinence, impotence, bleeding, infections and other undesirable secondary side-effects. He found it difficult to accept the potential impacts on his quality of life. At only sixty-six years old, he struggled with the reality of his diagnosis and the changes it might bring.

Lothar prepared for his prostate cancer operation in Australia with a mix of anxiety and hope. In the quiet of his darkened room, he found himself drifting in and out of sleep, the weight of his diagnosis heavy on his mind.

Suddenly, amidst the soft hum of the television, a voice broke through the fog of his drowsiness. He could distinctly hear the words,

"Prostate cancer, Loma Linda, Dr. Slater." The phrase resonated within him like a beacon of light. Startled yet curious, Lothar's eyes fluttered open. He squinted at the glowing screen, but the show was over. It felt like a divine intervention – an answer to his unspoken prayers for guidance in a time of uncertainty.

Driven by an instinctive urgency, Lothar reached for the book lying on his bedside table. Grabbing a pen, he quickly wrote down those key phrases – "Prostate cancer, Loma Linda, Dr. Slater" – across the cover. Each word felt like a lifeline, a potential path for healing.

The sleepiness that had overtaken him moments before faded, replaced by a newfound determination. Lothar felt compelled to research Dr Slater and the facility in Loma Linda California, hoping that this could be the turning point in his battle against prostate cancer.

That's when he discovered Loma Linda Medical Centre and their pioneering proton beam therapy. This innovative treatment promised precision without the collateral damage that other therapies brought. Encouraged by its success stories, Lothar felt a flicker of hope ignite within him.

His heart raced with a mix of excitement and trepidation as he prepared for his overseas call to Loma Linda in California. Armed with the key information he had hastily written down, he dialled the number, eager to secure his proton beam treatment. The voice on the other end was welcoming and informative, instantly putting him at ease. After discussing the options and confirming the derails of the treatment, he felt a surge of hope. The opportunity for a new beginning had presented itself. With his appointment set, Lothar turned his attention to arranging travel to the USA.

He quickly discovered that direct flights from Adelaide to Los Angeles were fully booked, a reality that made his heart sink momentarily. Fuelled by his new-found determination, he began scanning for alternative routes. After thoughtful consideration and several searches, he pieced together a series of connecting flights. This intricate journey involved multiple layovers – first to Sydney, then to Auckland New Zealand then to Honolulu, Hawaii and on to San Francisco, California, finally making his way to Los Angeles Airport.

Each segment of the trip was daunting, yet Lothar knew he had to reach Loma Linda within two days to keep his appointment. As the reality of the logistics set in, Lothar meticulously noted his flight schedule, ensuring he had ample time to make each connection.

While the prospect of the long journey felt overwhelming, a sense of purpose propelled him forward. On the day of departure, Lothar packed his bags with care, including the important documents for his treatment, a few personal belongings and a deep sense of determination. With his heart set on recovery, he embarked on an adventure that would take him across oceans, driven by the promise of healing that awaited him in Loma Linda Medical Centre in California.

What is Proton Therapy

Proton therapy for prostate cancer at Loma Linda University Medical Center in California is a cutting-edge treatment option that uses high-energy protons to target and destroy cancer cells while minimising damage to surrounding healthy tissues.

Proton therapy is a form of radiation treatment that utilizes protons - positively charged particles - to deliver precisely targeted doses of radiation to cancerous tumours. Unlike traditional X-ray radiation, which can pass through the body and affect healthy tissue beyond the tumour, protons release their energy directly at the tumour site. This is known as the Bragg peak effect.

Why Loma Linda?

Loma Linda University Medical Centre is a pioneer in proton therapy, having opened one of the world's first proton treatment facilities in 1990. The institution has a wealth of experience, having treated thousands of patients with various cancers, particularly prostate cancer.

Consultation
Patients undergo a thorough evaluation, which includes imaging and diagnostic tests to assess their cancer stage and overall health.

Simulation
A planning session involves detailed imaging, possibly including Magnetic Resonance Imaging (MRI) or Computed Tomography (CT) scans to precisely locate the tumour and ensure the right angles and dosage of treatment. Patients receive custom-made moulds to help them stay still during the procedure.

Treatment Planning
A team of radiation oncologists, medical physicists, and dosimetrists work together to develop a personalised treatment plan, determining the exact radiation dose and delivery techniques.

Treatment Sessions
Patients typically receive treatments five days a week over several weeks. Each session lasts about 30 minutes, and the actual proton delivery time is usually only a few minutes. Patients lie on a treatment table while a machine delivers protons precisely to the tumor.

Benefits of Proton Therapy
Proton therapy's precision helps spare surrounding healthy tissue and organs (like the bladder and rectum) from radiation exposure, potentially reducing side effects.

THE LAST HORIZON

Fewer Side Effects

Many patients report fewer long-term side effects compared to traditional radiation therapy. Common side effects can include fatigue, skin irritation, and temporary urinary symptoms, but many patients experience less severe impacts on their quality of life.

Lothar did not have any other side effects aside from skin irritation during the treatment.

Proton therapy at Loma Linda University Medical Center represents a progressive approach to treating prostate cancer, focusing on precision and patient care. With its long-standing reputation and specialised expertise, Loma Linda continues to be a leader in advancing cancer treatment methodologies, providing hope and healing for patients like Lothar, facing this challenging diagnosis.

With each session at Loma Linda, he was greeted by a supportive team who treated not just his illness but also his spirit. Three months passed and the transformative healing process lent him new vigour. As his treatment concluded, Lothar waited for the results, a mix of anxiety and hope flooding over him. The cancer was gone! Lothar felt an overwhelming wave of relief and gratitude. He had faced darkness and emerged into the light. With his health restored, Lothar embarked on a new chapter of his life, filled with renewed purpose.

When Lothar came back to Australia to get his annual check-ups, he found out that his Prostate-specific antigen (PSA) of 7.3 before the proton treatment had dropped to 0.026.

Grateful for his healing journey, Lothar transformed his experience with proton beam treatment into a powerful advocacy tool. He shared his journey, hoping to inspire others facing their own battles. He travelled, explored new passions, and most importantly, embraced each day with a profound appreciation he had never known before.

In the end, Lothar realised that his diagnosis had reshaped him –

not just as a survivor but as a man determined to live fully, cherishing every heartbeat and breath. He chose to redefine his story, proving that hope and resilience could carve new paths even in the face of daunting challenges.

Wisdom from a Book
Later in life, Lothar learned this excerpt full of wisdom from the book Unto Thee I Grant (Revised by Sri. Ramatherio a private, limited edition) written by Tibetan monk Lama Khemsar.

To a husband:
"Accept unto thyself a wife and obey the ordinance of God; take unto thyself a wife, and become a faithful member of society.

But examine with care and fix not suddenly.

On thy present choice depends thy future happiness.

If much of her time is destroyed in dress and adornments;

if she is enamoured with her own beauty, and delighted with her own praise; if she laugheth much, and talketh loud;

if her foot abideth not in her father's house,

though her beauty were as the sun in the firmament of heaven, turn thy face from her charms,

turn thy feet from her paths and suffer not thy mind to be ensnared by the allurements of imagination.

THE LAST HORIZON

But when thou findest sensibility of heart, joined with softness of manners,

an accomplished mind, with a form agreeable to thy fancy, take her home to thy house; she is worthy to be thy friend,

thy companion in life, the wife of thy bosom.

O cherish her, as a blessing sent thee from Heaven; let the kindness of thy behaviour endear thee to her heart.

She is the mistress of thy house;

treat her therefore with respect, that thy servants may obey her.

Oppose not her inclination without cause;

she is the partner of thy cares, make her also the companion of thy pleasures.

Reprove her faults with gentleness, exact not her obedience with rigour.

Trust thy secrets in her breast;

her counsels are sincere, thou shalt not be deceived.

Be faithful to her bed; for she is the mother of thy children. 'When pain and sickness assault her, let thy tenderness soothe her affliction;

a look from thee of pity and love shall alleviate her grief or mitigate her pain and be of more avail than ten physicians. Consider the tenderness of her sex, the delicacy of her frame; and be not severe to her weakness

but remember thine own imperfections."

The Essence of True Freedom: Standing Independent and Debt-Free

The connection between financial stability and our overall well-being is significant.

Lothar mulled over his beliefs about freedom – the kind that transcended mere absence of constraints. To him, genuine freedom meant the ability to stand on his own feet, to navigate life's challenges with a minimum reliance on others, except for computers, IT and electronic devices.

He relished the thought that every accomplishment, no matter how small, would be a testament to his capability and resilience. It wasn't just about being independent; it was about the strength that came from knowing he could carve out his own path in life.

The most important subject to Lothar was the notion of financial freedom. He believed this freedom meant being free from the burden of debt – whether it was owing money to friends, family, or the bank.

Lothar had always prided himself on being a responsible borrower. For forty-five years, he diligently paid his monthly amortisations to the bank, establishing a reputation as a loyal and dependable customer. Over the decades, he built a solid relationship with the institution, which he believed valued his commitment.

However, one day, without any prior notice, the bank demanded extra fees that Lothar felt was unjustified. This sudden imposition left him feeling betrayed and confused. After decades of faithful payments, the unexpected demand felt like a breach of trust.

Lothar wrestled with feelings of anger and frustration, convinced that the bank was attempting to take advantage of him. He struggled to reconcile his long-standing loyalty with this new treatment, believing he deserved better after all the years he had upheld his end of the bargain.

Determined to regain control of his life and finances, he made the difficult decision to sell his possessions. This act was not easy, but Lothar prioritised his goal of becoming debt-free. After successfully selling enough properties and belongings, he was able to pay off the bank, which alleviated a substantial burden from his shoulders.

With this newfound sense of freedom, Lothar focused intently on revitalising his business. His hard work and dedication paid off, and he began to earn money once again. As his financial situation improved, Lothar experienced a profound sense of relief, which translated into restful nights. No longer plagued by the stress of unpaid debts, he could finally enjoy peaceful sleep, knowing he was on the path to financial stability.

This journey taught him valuable lessons about resilience, the importance of managing debt and the rewards of hard work.

To him, financial stability represented a life where he could make choices without the weight of payments or loans hanging over his head. The idea of living within his means resonated deeply, fuelling a desire to work hard, save diligently, and invest wisely.

He could wake up each day without the gnawing anxiety of owing anyone anything- a life where he could own his possessions outright, free to invest in experiences, rather than repay debts.

This financial independence was intricately woven into his life of genuine freedom, where he could direct his life based on his values, passions and aspirations without external constraints.

Lothar was not only a labourer; he was a dreamer – the kind of man who believed that knowledge was power. Books became his refuge, a portal to understanding a world beyond his reach. With each turn of the page, he absorbed wisdom, learning from both triumphs and failures. He set up companies, one after another, resiliently rising from the ashes of setbacks.

These ventures became his testament to the strength of the human spirit. Yet, life was not without its heartaches. In the embrace of love, he found joy, but the inevitable pangs of heartbreak followed.

Nevertheless, he persisted, ever eager to make his mark in an unfamiliar world. Now, at the remarkable age of eighty-six, he stands tall – a monument of a life well-lived. Debt-free and rich in spirit, Lothar reflects on the tapestry of his existence, woven from experience and resilience.

Though the years have etched their lines upon his face, they tell stories of grit, determination, and unyielding hope. In a world that often values youth, he remains a testament to the strength found in experience. He has cultivated a life of productivity, every day an opportunity to learn, to teach, and to grow.

As he looks toward the horizon, Lothar lives with the resolve to continue working until his last breath, embodying the essence of a warrior who has weathered many storms – his heart, though burdened, beats steadily with purpose. In this journey to the twilight of his years, he carries with him the lessons of a lifetime, a living testament that life, with all its trials, can indeed be a beautiful adventure.

Lothar is a testament to resilience and perseverance, having navigated a myriad of challenges throughout his life. Growing up, he faced the difficulties of a tumultuous childhood that tested his spirit and determination. Yet, with unwavering resolve, Lothar emerged from those early struggles, shaping his character and fortifying his will. As he transitioned into adulthood, the quest for meaningful employment presented its own set of obstacles. Lothar tirelessly sought job opportunities, exhibiting a tenacity that ultimately led him to find roles that matched his skills and ambitions, despite the fierce competition he faced.

Education was another hurdle in Lothar's journey. His formal education was but a flicker – a few years in the classroom, quickly overshadowed by the harsher realities of life yet he sought knowledge wherever he could, often relying on self-education and life experiences to enrich his understanding of the world.

As the tides of conflict rose, he ventured far and wide, embracing any job that came his way to earn a modest living. Lothar relied on his physical strength, forging a path through adversity with each determined step.

Financial constraints were a constant companion during his early years, compelling Lothar to make tough choices and often prioritise essentials over luxuries. Yet, through hard work and resilience, he gradually improved his financial situation, learning to manage his resources wisely.

Perhaps the most formidable challenge Lothar faced was his battle with prostate cancer. This health crisis tested his physical and mental strength, but Lothar's fighting spirit shone brightly as he sought unconventional treatment and paramount support, ultimately emerging with a renewed appreciation of life.

Now, as he navigates the challenges that come with old age, Lothar remains undeterred. He continues to embrace life with vigour and determination, adopting a lifestyle focused on health and well-being. He engages in regular exercise; - yoga, swimming, walking. He maintains a balanced diet, eating more vegetables and fruits every day, and cherishes connections with family and friends.

Lothar's desire to live a long and fulfilling life fuels his every action. With each passing day, he confronts the realities of aging while holding onto hope and ambition. His journey is a powerful reminder of human resilience and the unyielding pursuit of a life well-lived, showing that despite the obstacles, the spirit to thrive can lead one to live a hundred vibrant years.

He believes that the 'Great Architect of the Universe' will give him the desires of his heart as promised in Psalms 37:4 in the Holy Bible. As Lothar turned eighty-six years old in 2024, he realised that life has just begun and is looking forward to being a centenarian in 2038.

In Lothar's eyes, each day is a new horizon, and he intends to fill it with purpose and joy, celebrating the beauty of being alive and active until he faces the last horizon.

Medal Pick & Shovel Carbide lamp

Some of Lothar's Paintings

"Melodies of a Rainy Afternoon in Paris" *"Scarlet Streak Across the Night"*

THE LAST HORIZON

" *Street of Timeless Charm*" "*Cradle of Creation*"

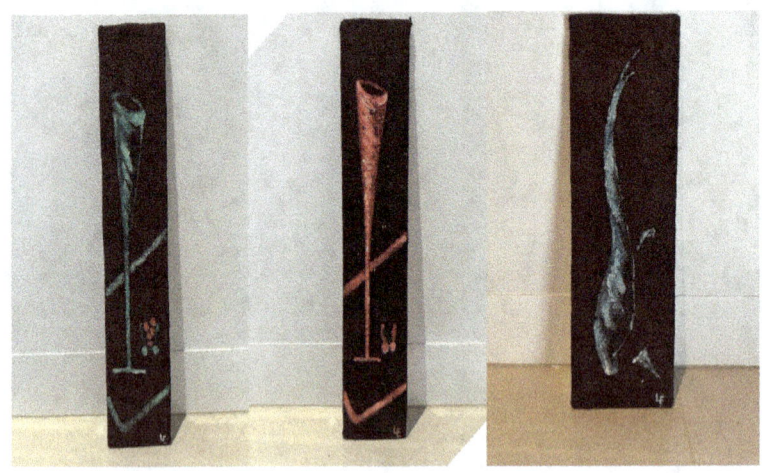

"*Elysian Intrigue*" "*Crimson Fizz*" "*Azure Allure*"

MAGGIE CUDANIN EBBINGHAUS

Wolfgang and Sue Doser – Bill Doser – Else Doser

Helga, Mark, Lothar & Pierre in 1967

Lothar @ 86

AUTHOR'S NOTES: THE MAP IN NAVIGATING LIFE'S CHALLENGES

The ultimate benefit of a map is its ability to provide clarity and navigation, making it an indispensable tool in various contexts. To minimise the risk of getting lost in navigating life's challenges, please use THE MAP.

T for Time H for Health E for Experience

M for Money A for Age P for Purpose.

Time, Love and Attention

Time spent together with family and friends is irreplaceable; it builds strong bonds and creates lasting memories. Engaging in family activities, helping with homework or simply having dinner together fosters meaningful connections that money cannot buy. Love and attention are equally crucial.

These aspects help nurture a family's emotional health. Children thrive in environments where they feel valued and prioritised. A simple gesture, like sitting down to talk about their day, or showing affection through hugs and words of encouragement, reinforces feelings of love and security.

Moreover, respect forms the foundation of all healthy relationships within the family. Treating family members with kindness, valuing their opinions, and fostering an environment of mutual respect builds a sense of safety and acceptance. This respectful atmosphere nurtures open communication, allowing family members to express themselves freely and creating a sense of belonging.

Health
Health is number one in life. Physical, mental and emotional health empowers us to do what we enjoy and allows us to savour the moments that bring fulfillment. By prioritising our well-being, we pave the way for a more vibrant and enriched existence, filled with activities that ignite our passions and bring joy to our lives. Embracing a healthy lifestyle is not just a choice; it's a fundamental investment in our happiness and the quality of our experiences.

Experience: Your Greatest Asset
Experience – something that cannot be taught or bought. This accumulated knowledge and insight is a powerful tool that can be leveraged in countless ways. Whether it's mentoring younger generations, writing a memoir, or leading a community initiative, your life experiences can provide invaluable contributions to society. Mentorship is a role that benefits greatly from experience. Sharing the lessons you've learned over decades can help guide others on their own journeys, offering them the wisdom that only comes from having lived through similar challenges.

Money
Money is a tool that can provide the security we need to pursue our as-

pirations, alleviate stress and foster positive relationships. While it's essential to recognise that money alone does not define happiness, having a stable financial foundation allows us to focus on what truly matters in life, creating a sense of balance and fulfillment in our daily experiences. Financial stability offers us the freedom to thrive, establishing the groundwork for a stable and rewarding life.

Promoting the wise use of money while cautioning against the worship of it, leads to a healthier, more fulfilling life. By understanding its value as a tool rather than an idol, individuals achieve financial stability while focusing on what genuinely brings joy and purpose to their lives.

Use money wisely:
- Understand the value of money – Money is a tool. Recognize that it holds value, but it is not an end in itself.
- Budgeting - Track income and expenses. Save for emergencies. Save now for your retirement
- Invest in experiences, not just possessions – Spending money on experiences can lead to lasting memories and personal growth
- Practice mindful spending - considering needs over wants and evaluate the long-term impact of purchases
- Build wealth with purpose – view money as a means to achieve meaningful goals.
- Financial Education – knowledge about managing money, investing and saving wisely empowers individuals to make informed decisions rather than being driven by a desire for more wealth.
- Positivity Towards Giving - money should be used to uplift others. Give with a happy heart.

Age as a Catalyst for Productivity

Age should never be used as an alibi to avoid being productive. Instead, it should be seen as a catalyst – a stage of life where you can combine your experience, wisdom and passions to continue making meaningful contributions. The world needs the unique perspectives and talent that come with age. So, rather than stepping back, step forward and embrace the possibilities that lie ahead. You are never too old to be productive, to learn, to create, or to make a difference.

As the years go by, it's easy to slip into the mindset that age is a barrier to productivity. The narrative that aging automatically leads to a decline in capability or purpose is not only limiting but also false. Age can be a power ally, bringing with it experience, wisdom and a deeper understanding on what truly matters. Rather than using age as an excuse to step back, it's time to view it as a reason to step up – to harness your life's experiences and continue contributing meaningfully to the world around you.

Purpose
Having a sense of purpose is essential at any stage of life, but it becomes even more crucial as you age. Purpose drives action and provides motivation, giving you a reason to get up in the morning and stay engaged with life. Whether your purpose is tied to your family, community, or personal goals, it's important to continue nurturing it as you grow old.

"When you help others to shine, your joy becomes divine."
Maggie Cudanin Ebbinghaus
Author

German Vocabulary Used	English Translation
Passampt	Passport Office
Eintopf	Lentil stew
Errinerung an die erste grubenfahrt	Memory of the first descent

ACKNOWLEDGMENT

Photo credits and thanks to the following websites:

Alchetron – the free social encyclopedia for the photo of Castel Felice

The couple Ella and Ariel Gad for the photos of their local sailboat 'paraw' in Boracay Island, Malay, Aklan, Philippines

Thank you www.llu.edu for the proton therapy information

Thank you www.britannica.com/event/Marshall-Plan for The Marshall Plan excerpt

Thank you Wikipedia the free encyclopedia and National Museum of Australia (NMA) for the Post War Australian Migration information

Thank you The Rosicrucian Order AMORC

https://rosicrucian.org Rosicrucian books unto-thee-I-grant for the excerpt 'To A Husband' from the book 'Unto Thee I Grant

Thank you www.history.com/war/topics for some information about the World War 11 Germany

www.ingramcontent.com/pod-product-compliance
Lightning Source LLC
Chambersburg PA
CBHW052144070526
44585CB00017B/1971